All That's Gone and Still Remains: Reflections of a Man at Midlife

Essays on the Opportunities, Challenges, Hopes and Fears of Midlife

By Adam Gordon Sachs

Essays Available on the Midlife Dude Blog:
www.MidlifeDude.Wordpress.com

Also by Adam Gordon Sachs under Sirenian Publishing imprint:

- ❖ *Don't Knock, He's Dead: A Longshot Candidate Gets Schooled in the Unseemly Underbelly of American Campaign Politics*

- ❖ *Three Yards and a Plate of Mullet*

Our greatest sin may be choosing to remain unconscious, in spite of all the evidence that mounts through the years that other elements within us are actively making choices on our behalf, often with disastrous consequences...To engage with the summons of our souls is to step into the deepest ocean, uncertain whether we will be able to swim to some new, distant shore. And yet, until we have consented to swim beyond the familiar lights of the port left behind, we will never arrive at a newer shore. For some, the entry is gradual; others are pushed suddenly into deep waters.

James Hollis, *Finding Meaning in the Second Half of Life: How to Finally, Really Grow Up*

Meaninglessness inhibits fullness of life and is therefore equivalent to illness. Meaning makes a great many things endurable – perhaps everything.

Carl Jung, *Memories, Dreams, Reflections*

In a world, man must create his own essence: it is in throwing himself into the world, suffering there, struggling there, that he gradually defines himself.

Jean-Paul Sartre, *Characterizations of Existentialism*

People prefer the certainty of misery to the misery of uncertainty.

Virginia Satir, author and therapist

If one has refused to budge through the midlife transition, the sense of staleness will calcify into resignation. One by one, the safety and supports will be withdrawn from the person who is standing still. Parents will become children; children will become strangers; a mate will grow away or go away; the career will become just a job—and each of those events will be felt as an abandonment....the jolt may be just what is needed to prod the resigned middle-ager toward seeking revitalization...If we have confronted ourselves in the middle passage, and found a renewal of purpose around which we are eager to build a more authentic life structure, these may well be the best years.

Gail Sheehy, Passages: Predictable Crises of Adult Life

Acknowledgements

I want to acknowledge my children, Rebecca and Daniel Sachs, who were the inspiration for some of these essays, taught me all I know about parenting, and who will always be the most important people in my life; my father, Lyle Sachs, who has been the most loyal reader and commenter on my Midlife Dude blog; my wife, Amy Grossman Sachs, for being my biggest and most loyal supporter through my rollercoaster ride of midlife and who knows better than anyone else the happenings about which I write; and my late mother, Sandra Sachs, the inspiration for my attempted longshot political career who always encouraged my writing.

All That's Gone and Still Remains: Reflections of a Man at Midlife

Essays on the Opportunities, Challenges, Hopes and Fears of Midlife

CONTENTS

All That's Gone and Still Remains: Reflections of a Man at Midlife

Essays on the Opportunities, Challenges, Hopes and Fears of Midlife

Introduction

Midlife and Crisis: An Uneasy Relationship

Midlife gets a bad rap. What else can be concluded when "midlife" is practically married to "crisis?" Two peas in a pod they are, "midlife" and "crisis." But are they really well matched?

Canadian psychologist Elliott Jaques coined the term "midlife crisis" in 1965, concluding in a study that creative geniuses underwent changes of style or declines in productivity in their mid-to-late-30s. The term gained traction in popular culture by the 1970s, describing the time of life roughly between ages 40 and 65 when adults become attuned to their own mortality, concerned with leaving a mark before dying, and reflective about whether their first half of life has been meaningful.

But the term has snowballed from its origins documenting the imaginative processes of artists and poets in an obscure, dry journal of psychoanalysis to represent everything cataclysmic that seemingly afflicts the middle-aged trying desperately to ignore failed dreams and roll back the merciless tide of aging in a culture fixated on youth.

Author Gail Sheehy cemented the gloomy view of midlife in her landmark 1976 bestselling book, *Passages: Predictable Crises of Adult Life*, referring to decades of life as the "Forlorn Forties" and "Resigned Fifties."

Time to Ditch Wife for Bombshell?

"Midlife crisis" is more typically applied to males, at least when couched in a derogatory manner signifying an unofficial malady.

"Midlife crisis" has come to denote the man who ditches his long-devoted, slightly wrinkling and graying wife for the platinum blonde bombshell 20 years his junior in his office; trades in his practical suburban family vehicle for the candy-apple red Porsche roadster; and transforms from dull and predictable to flamboyant and impulsive, fueled by a surge of drugging and boozing in a pathetic effort to recapture the carefree, raucous days of yore.

For women, the term "midlife crisis" generally carries an undertone that is more forgiving and socially validating, one tilted more toward liberation than debauchery. Sure, some midlife women succumb to vain attempts to recapture youth through medical and cosmetic procedures, or irresponsibly abandon a family to engage in self-indulgent, feel-good, self-destructive behaviors.

The 40s decade certainly seems a marker of heightened vulnerability and confusion for women, as the beauty of youth wanes, marriages grow stale and risk of divorce increase, and children become more independent and leave, diminishing what many women regard as a primary raison d'etre.

Yet, midlife is characterized more as a time of renewal, rebirth and exploration for women. It is seen as an opportunity to shed an old self that may have been contorted to meet societal, cultural, marital and parental expectations and transform into a more authentic, independent, self-accepting, self-confident being, and to reclaim aspects of personality and passions lost along the way.

Midlife is viewed as a period of re-evaluation and adjustment, of increased wisdom, strengths, experience and vitality, when old dreams that no longer inspire are abandoned and more genuine desires and talents take hold, a process known as self-actualization, or becoming more fully oneself. Rather than a "crisis" producing angst, depression and dissatisfaction, psychotherapist and author Stephanie Marston declared that the women she chronicled in her book, *If Not Now, When? Reclaiming Ourselves at Midlife,* characterized midlife as "one of the best times of their lives."

What's the Crisis?

Social science researchers have varied widely on whether any identifiable phenomenon that could be labeled as "midlife crisis" exists; numerous studies have shown midlife is not characterized by pervasive crises. Certainly, there are no commonly defined symptoms and nothing resembling a midlife disorder appears in the Bible of mental health, the Diagnostic and Statistical Manual of Mental Disorders.

Count renowned psychologist Daniel Levinson, author of the 1978 seminal book, *Seasons of a Man's Life,* among the true believers. Following a group of working men for 10 years, Levinson developed a theory that delineated adulthood as a series of stages and transitions, each with a developmental task or crisis to resolve to advance to the next stage with a sense of well-being.

Unlike some other researchers who rejected the concept of a "midlife crisis," Levinson determined that 80 percent of the men he interviewed found the midlife transition a tumultuous struggle and psychologically painful. He bluntly described the existential predicament men face at midlife in *Seasons*: "Adults hope that life begins at 40 – but the great anxiety is that it ends there...It is terrifying to go through middle age in the shadow of death...and it is a self-defeating illusion to live it in the shadow of youth..."

I believe the stereotypical male version of a "midlife crisis" is overblown, hyperbole, a caricature. In reality, I contend a man's "midlife crisis" more closely resembles the woman's experience of re-evaluation, greater self-knowledge and wisdom – at least among those adults who aren't withering in place – than the stereotypical jerk wearing shiny new bling glinting through an open shirt, cruising in an eye-popping Corvette convertible, ditzy blonde under his arm, toupee blowing in the wind.

Midlife Challenges

Midlife requires leaps of faith, acceptance and tolerance of uncertainty. We encounter the realization that our careers may have hit a ceiling, and re-evaluate whether the work at which we might have labored for decades provides meaning or nourishes our soul anymore, or ever did. We pause to question whether the race for success, advancement and achievement, as defined in young adulthood, is worth chasing anymore.

If we haven't already experienced job loss through no fault of our own, we are prime targets for downsizing and early retirement packages because of our age and salaries. We have to run ever faster to avoid becoming obsolete in the face of rapid societal and technological changes, the province of the young.

We grapple with the financial pressures of mortgages, college tuitions, accumulated debt, material acquisitions, increasing health care costs and looming retirement. We question whether our marriages are satisfying or have gone flat, whether the grass may be greener.

We groom our children and ultimately set them free – except those suffering from Failure to Launch Syndrome -- experiencing some sense of loss entering the childless phase. We may be sandwiched, caring for ailing parents while parenting our own kids. Mounting midlife challenges can be associated with high levels of stress, anxiety and sadness, which can lead to unhealthy lifestyles, deterioration of physical and mental health and acceleration of aging.

Through it all, we face choices, the biggest of which is whether we will transition at this crossroad toward reimagining and reinvigorating a life with new possibilities, purpose and contributions through continued growth and development, or whether we will hunker down, circle the wagons, kick like a mule, pull the covers tight, switch on autopilot and hang on mightily to the status quo, resigned to becoming a member of the walking dead until the nursing home comes calling.

Giving Back vs. Giving Up

Psychologist Erik Erickson captured this dichotomous phase of life in his preeminent Stages of Psychosocial Development theory, identifying midlife as the period of Generativity vs. Stagnation. Adults entering their second half of life would either help guide the next generation through socially valuable work, creativity, productivity and loving relationships, or would stagnate in a pool of self-centeredness and ineffectiveness. Those who do not associate change with growth but rather with loss, being passed by or failing are destined to weigh on Erickson's Stagnation side of the scale.

I have dealt with many of midlife's rites of passage. I have lost jobs multiple times; changed careers, requiring a return to school and sacrificing years of experience in other fields and more money to start over in an occupation that stirred my soul; moved to experience a new environment and culture; divorced and remarried; faced the challenges of parenting teen-aged kids and watched them leave home for independent lives; cared for an ailing mother, and lost her; observed a colleague succumb to the ravages of alcohol and depression; experienced a major health setback and long rehabilitation; and strived for self-fulfilling goals involving creative expression.

I believe I'm heading down Erickson's path of Generativity; if I wasn't, I imagine my life would be crushingly bland and I would be miserable, jaded and bitter.

These essays, compiled upon my entry into and over the course of a clinical mental health counseling graduate program from my late 40s to mid-50s, provide commentary from a personal perspective on these and other midlife issues, and seek to relate my experiences broadly to others going through similar midlife transitional phases and events.

These writings reflect the opportunities and challenges, risks and rewards, hopes and fears, and triumphs and setbacks I've experienced and observed in midlife.

In tone, the essays are inspirational, triumphant, motivational, hopeful, wistful, prideful, contemplative, philosophical, inquisitive, wondrous, humorous, melancholic, depressing, upsetting, mournful, resigned, raw, disappointed, critical, self-questioning – in short, the kaleidoscope that the midlife passage presents to our minds, hearts and souls.

CHAPTER 1

Nostalgic for Youth

Man at Midlife

My wife has been talking recently about planning my 50th birthday party. For Chrissake, I'm still just 48! Let's not rush it. I really don't want to think about it. It shocks me. But it's going to happen (I certainly hope). When I think about my younger self, 50 seems really old, like that's not just my dad, it's nearly my grandpa! I've noticed myself becoming a lot more nostalgic in the last few years. So many things remind me of childhood or college or my bachelor days. Part of the nostalgia is the feeling that back then, way back then, I was free, unencumbered, with limitless possibilities and limited responsibilities. Now, of course, it's totally different.

I don't feel 48. I'm in good shape physically. I play recreational soccer with people half my age, and can at least hold my own. I'm pretty sure I'm the oldest player in the league, which numbers about 200 players. Sometimes getting beat by a young gun makes me contemplate retirement from the game, but it's the one thing that reminds me most of being a kid and it's too much fun, so I keep re-upping for another season. I played varsity tennis in college and still compete in high-level leagues, and can give younger players a good battle. I run to stay in shape. It used to be easier. I'm feeling the effects of age on my stamina.

My daughter is preparing for the SAT and is a year-and-a-half from college. She's got her driver learner's permit. I remember her keeping me up all night with colicky crying. I can see her becoming a young woman. I'm trying to get used to the idea of letting her go...gradually.

I'm pretty sure at least half my life is over, unless I can become one of those Centenarians featured on the Today Show. I'm terrified of the older years, so I want to make sure I leave everything on the table now. From day to day, that seems hard to do, but that is real life. By coincidence, I attended a funeral today of a co-worker who died suddenly one day last week -- didn't even make it home from work. She made it to the parking garage, had trouble breathing, an ambulance was summoned, and the next day, her desk was empty. Made me think you can never be sure you'll make it home again.

I'll write about my life and thoughts as I go through this midlife period, now as an experienced parent whose kids still need him, but not as much, as a mid-career man of modest success who is still searching for that passion, as a second-time husband still trying to get marriage right, as a new graduate student who graduated college more than half a life ago. I hope and expect you'll find something of yourself in these reflections.

Nostalgia for the Chevrolet Corvair – and Youth

There's something about certain cars that causes me to immerse in a wave of nostalgia.

Today while doing an errand, strolling through a parking lot full of late model SUVs, sedans and minivans, I came upon a 1966 Chevrolet Corvair Corsa that stopped me in my tracks.

I'm not a gearhead by any means and know relatively little about cars. But I love certain iconic cars that remind me of my youth, from the late 1960s through the 1970s: the Ford Pinto, Ford Maverick and Ford Mustang; the AMC Gremlin, AMC Pacer (introduced to later generations as the *Wayne's World* car) and AMC Javelin; the Chevy Vega, Chevy Camaro and Chevy Nova; the VW Beetle and VW Karmann Ghia; the Dodge Dart Swinger and Dodge Challenger; the Mercury Cougar; the Oldsmobile Cutlass Supreme; the Opel Manta and the Pontiac Le Mans. I collected Matchbox cars as a kid – that may account for some of my fascination.

The look of the Corvair always intrigued me, and I don't know why. It looks almost like a sports car, but not quite. It's got the unusual four headlights in front, like an extra set of eyes, and four little round red tail lights in back, like flashing doughnuts. Its body seems really flat and low to the ground. It's just cool. And you rarely see them on the roads these days.

As I snapped a photo and stood to admire the old-timer in a sea of infants, the owner approached and began talking to me. He must have been accustomed to people stopping to examine his car.

He told me he owned three Corvairs, including one he originally purchased in 1965. The model he was driving this day was an Aztec rust-colored 1966 Corvair Corsa that he purchased about 25 years ago from a farmer who advertised the car for sale on his property. We talked for about five minutes about the novelty of driving a 50-year-old Corvair today, and how the model gained national attention when consumer protection advocate Ralph Nader went on a crusade claiming the Corvair was unsafe.

Some of my fascination also is plain nostalgia for my youth, when times seemed simpler, when I felt more free, unbound by the typical worries, responsibilities, expectations and pressures of adulthood.

Whenever I see NFL Films footage from the 1960s and 1970s, the slow motion football shots with grass flying and players grimacing inside helmets, with the symphonic music, it immediately takes me back to that more innocent time.

In my early 50s, I have become more nostalgic not so much for my boyhood youth, but for the most carefree time of my adulthood, my *relative youth,* when I transitioned from my frigid upstate New York college to the palm trees and sunshine of Gulf Coast Florida.

I moved back to the Northeast after two years, but frequently find myself reminiscing about the more laid-back, tropical environment I experienced. Recently I've been pondering making a return to a similar, more casual and warmer region from the busier, fast-paced, colder Northeast.

Seeing the Corvair brings me back in time, just like my memories of living on a barrier island on the Gulf of Mexico at 23, drinking beers with friends on the seawall behind our rental bungalow.

The Corvair is frozen in time – a decade of production ceased in 1969 – but I'm not. I have to examine whether my yearning is merely nostalgia or something in my gut telling me that something more nourishing for my spirit is beckoning me on the horizon.

Reliving Youth

May 24, 2016 -- Tomorrow I leave home for my summer job. It feels like I'm back in college, when I worked one summer in Nantucket, MA and another in Los Angeles. Except now I'm 53.

I'll be working as a seasonal tennis pro at the Sea Colony Tennis resort in Bethany Beach, DE. I already had a taste of the resort tennis teaching life for my first long weekend in May. It was a welcome break from the career grind and mundane office environment.

This summer's job reflects the saying, "Necessity is the mother of invention." It certainly was not part of a long-term plan, but born out of necessity to change course, re-imagine life and re-adjust on the fly in response to circumstances.

At midlife, I'm embracing the idea that life does not have to be lived only one way. You can have a grind-it-out, 40-hour per week job, year-in and year-out. Or you can find another way to make a living in this Gig Economy, while trying to steal back more time, flexibility and independence. And with that, more purpose, meaning and passion.

I'm also embracing the philosophy of minimalism, or at least trying to limit my spending, cut costs, reduce my income needs and live a simplified life that maximizes enjoyment and meaning and minimizes stress. That's what this summer will be all about.

My full-time employment in public relations ended in October 2015, for various reasons, and not voluntarily.

One was that reality sunk in about the challenges performing a full-time job, working a part-time internship in a new field as a counselor at an outpatient mental health clinic, and taking graduate school classes in counseling, not to mention trying to function as a father and husband. I soon realized that trying to do all of these would be to do them all half-assed, and be constantly exhausted and over-stressed. My job had gone south anyway, so the break was a relief.

But I left that job with no clear plan on how to produce income while I completed the final two years of my counseling program, including two intensive year-long internships. I fell back on teaching tennis, which I had done during previous job layoffs. I was lucky to pick up weekend hours with a Baltimore-based tennis academy.

Then the idea occurred to me: Why not apply to resorts that need additional instructors for busy summer tennis seasons, while I was in between semesters with no internship or classes? With the help of a good connection, I landed the Sea Colony position.

I'm looking forward to it. It should be a great summer. Being at the beach in a resort town, working outside doing something fun, working with a team that has a passion for tennis, getting paid to help people improve at what they enjoy, meeting many people, making new friends. Hard to beat that, and sure as hell beats sitting at a desk in a stuffy office staring at a computer screen for eight hours a day.

Of course, it won't be all fun and games. I need to make money to fund me and my wife's living, my education and my two kids' college educations. So I'll have to hustle and promote myself to line up as many private lessons and clinics as I can, in addition to the many clinics the resort schedules every day. That should be great practice for the when I become a counselor with an independent practice.

A friend referred to this time in my life – a summer teaching tennis sandwiched by counseling internships, classes and part-time jobs with no full-time job as an anchor – as a "reset." It sure feels like a step back in time for me, all the way to the relatively more carefree and low stress days of college.

Make no mistake, there's some scrambling and anxiousness involved. But I'm grateful for the respite, happy, excited about the challenges, and optimistic about the future. You can't *really* relive your youth, but if you can add some youthful exuberance and new experiences to your life – and even some motivating uncertainty -- you can recapture some of those feelings. And that's healthy at any age.

CHAPTER 2

Life Changes:
Shaking Things Up

Ch-Ch-Ch-Ch-Changes:
The Midlife Transition

At midlife, I'm in transition…constantly.

Over the last year, in my early 50s, I've faced more challenging transitions than any other year of my life. It keeps me always somewhat on edge.

My life has been like a David Bowie song, minus the stutter:

Ch-Ch-Ch-Ch-Changes
Turn and face the strain…

As my kids reached the ages of 20 and 18 and I pursued a second career change, I have:

- ❖ Left a full-time job in public relations after seven years, been unemployed and learned to live without a steady paycheck
- ❖ Become a full-time graduate student
- ❖ Scrambled to find part-time work, even trying out as a "coach" for a company that teaches soccer and educational skills to pre-school kids, something out of my element

* Completed an internship in a new field, mental health counseling (therapy)
* Adopted, to some degree, the minimalism approach to life
* Switched from graduate school and the counseling internship to a six-day-per-week job as a tennis instructor for the late spring and summer months for a much-needed cash infusion
* Moved from the D.C.-Baltimore suburbs to a Delaware beach town to work as a seasonal tennis instructor
* Transitioned from married and family life to bachelorhood, living with two single roommates for my summer hiatus at the tennis resort
* Adapted to an empty nest, with one child in college and another entering this fall
* Acknowledged that my 20-year-old daughter really has become an independent adult, observing her navigate a semester abroad in France and travel around Europe

It's been a lot of change for one year; most of it was of my own volition and some of it was thrust upon me. Overall, encountering transitions has been positive, though sometimes admittedly nerve-racking. It has kept me motivated, challenged and stimulated. One thing's for sure: I have never been bored or complacent during this transitory period.

The transitions have required me to look within and summon my confidence and belief in myself, which has been something I've often struggled with. I've had to do this on a daily basis in both my counseling internship and tennis teaching job, working in environments that were completely unfamiliar and in positions where I've had to project confidence immediately with strangers.

The transitions will keep unfolding. I expect to graduate with the counseling degree in May 2017, and then embark on the new career for real, but in what capacity, I'm not sure. My son will move out for good to his campus dorm in August. I'm even thinking of moving from the area I've lived for the past 28 years to a smaller locale in the South, as I transition to the new career and seek a warmer, slower-paced, more gracious lifestyle more befitting of the minimalist philosophy.

Transitions have been healthy for me. At a time of midlife when many may be stagnating and biding time until a retirement of unknown purpose and activity, I feel optimistic and excited about my future and the opportunities and meaning transitions will bring.

For anyone contemplating a meaningful transition in midlife, I recommend taking the risk, or you may regret missing your window down the road.

Is the Grass Greener?

I typically believe the grass is greener on the other side, just over the next hill. It may be self-delusional or wishful thinking, but it's my nature, however torturous it can be, to believe there's something better.

Such thinking can be the curse of people who are never satisfied with life and what they have, always seeking, never arriving. Or it can be the motivation that leads to risk-taking, improvement and growth.

I have been seeking greener grass in my career through a marathon five-year journey, and now that I'm on the brink of making a transition from public relations to mental health counseling after what will be 22 graduate courses and two years of internships -- and one collapsed full-time job along with its reliable income under all that weight -- I am pretty confident that the fescue indeed will be brighter.

I also have been thinking that as I launch my new career in 2017 – which will include, ideally and ultimately, my own independent practice – that a new geographic location may offer greener pastures than the Baltimore-Washington megalopolis where I have been stationed for 28 years, business-, lifestyle-, scenery- and culture-wise.

My thinking is that the time to make a geographic change would coincide with my career transition, or at least relatively early in my new career, before becoming established in one place.

I also will be 54, far into midlife, by the time I graduate the counseling program. If I go somewhere else, I want to be young enough to become engaged in the fabric of the new community occupationally, socially, civically, recreationally and other ways, not just to live out retirement (which I don't know if I will ever want to reach anyway).

I have already had people advise me against moving, telling me essentially that the grass *is not* greener, that the desire for something fresh and new is merely a cover for a compulsion to escape.

The idea of moving is complicated by several factors, primarily family concerns. Some factors I believe are manageable: I don't have a big fear of change; the move wouldn't necessarily be irreversible if it didn't work out; I believe I could make new friends and keep old ones with some effort; I am confident I can earn a living and be successful starting a business.

But family, that is the hardest one to gauge. I'm a new empty-nester. Both of my kids are attending Maryland colleges. My daughter will graduate the same weekend I will in 2017. She may go to France to teach English; she may follow her boyfriend to an engineering job in Texas or beyond; or she may stay in Maryland. My son will have at least two years left. My extended family is small and scattered.

My wife's family and her roots are in Maryland. She doesn't want to leave. I understand. Many would argue that factor alone should kibosh the whole idea. And perhaps it will. Or perhaps there could be room for compromise and negotiation as events unfold and more is discovered.

There's no doubt that the belief that the grass could be greener can complicate life and cause angst. But it's also a belief that gives those prone to seeking an excitement about the unknown, about a new experience, about what could be around that next corner, over that next hill. Will it be emerald green, or drought-baked brown?

Ramblin' Man

November 2017 -- For the second time in my adult life, I loaded all my possessions I could fit in a compact car and traveled more than 500 miles to a new city in a new state to begin a new career and concomitantly, a new life.

Two small differences were that the first time, I drove a Honda Civic from Washington, D.C. to Florida; the second time, a Toyota Corolla from Maryland to South Carolina.

A bigger difference is that the first time I was 22 and just starting out in life, the future stretched out before me like the unending Eastern Seaboard expanse of Interstate 95 that I trekked to Florida, with few obligations or attachments. If the world wasn't yet exactly my oyster, I had what seemed an eternity to search for pearls.

This time, I was 54, acutely aware of entering the latter stages of my career and wanting to make it inspired, with long-standing financial, material, family, friendship and community ties from nearly three decades in the Baltimore-Washington region.

Quite simply, there was more riding on my decision – more people to potentially disappoint or who would disapprove; more things to give up; a sense of security and stability that comes with comfort and familiarity to be shattered; greater doubts and fears about starting anew in midlife to be conquered.

Moving is never easy, especially when relocating as far away as I have, from Maryland to the Charleston area of South Carolina, far enough to truly be gone. I feel like I've made a highly unconventional decision to upend my life at this midlife stage, gone against the grain. Indeed, demographic studies and surveys say I have.

While the United States is widely viewed as a land of boundless geographic mobility, with its heritage of explorers braving the Wild West frontiers and searching for their fortune in gold, the truth is, many Americans never venture more than a half-hour from their hometowns to live. Most Americans, especially from certain demographic groups, are stayers, not movers.

- ❖ A 2015 University of Michigan Health and Retirement Study found that the typical adult – half the population -- lives within 18 miles of his or her mother, and only 20 percent live more than a few hours' drive from their parents. The study showed that over the last few decades, Americans are staying put at higher rates, with multiple generations remaining close to relatives for financial and logistical support. Those with college educations and higher incomes are more likely to live farther from their parents.

- ❖ A 2015 Allstate/NATIONAL JOURNAL Heartland Monitor poll determined that more than half of respondents lived in close proximity to where they grew up. The percentage of stayers was highest for people from rural areas and small towns. Nearly half of all respondents had lived in the same area for 21 years or more. The pull to stay put is

> strong: Less than half of the respondents who believed that their hometown regions were on the downswing economically nevertheless said that the possibility of a move was not likely for them.

❖ A 2008 Pew Research Center survey found that nearly 40 percent of Americans had never left the hometown region in which they were born, and 57 percent had never lived in a state other than the state in which they were born. Those who moved most often cited greater economic opportunity; the main influencers for stayers were family, established connections, and a sense of belonging.

Anecdotally, it seemed to me that people in my demographic group – college educated suburban or urban dwellers -- moved around in early adulthood as they established careers, sought better opportunities, climbed work and social ladders and started families. But once they entered that next stage, middle adulthood, they seemed to stay put for decades until retirement, in their 60s or 70s, or beyond.

Beyond the pull of family, connections, familiarity and a sense of belonging, a big reason few people move in midlife is that it's just plain hard, especially emotionally. It's a gamble, as much as one tries to predict and reduce the risk through analysis, projection and planning. I'm experiencing that now, just completing the first two weeks in my adopted new South Carolina hometown. Everything is new; nothing is known. I can't sit back and wait for things to happen; I have to make them happen. It takes energy, effort and openness. It requires being outgoing, to meet new people, forge relationships with work colleagues and get involved in things I like to do. It involves learning and adapting to a new culture – as my boss jokes: "get used to guns and fried chicken."

It can be lonely – extremely lonely. I relocated to a region where I have no friends or family. Some may call this decision a mistake, a dumb move, a misguided effort to search for where "the grass is greener."

I certainly have misgivings. I have given up a lot, and that weighs on me. I still don't know how some things will turn out because of my decision.

I almost abandoned the idea of moving many times, but an urge wouldn't let me. I made a gut decision based on seeking a change of environment after 30 years; an opportunity where I would perhaps be a larger fish in a smaller pond in my new counseling career, thus increasing business prospects; and a place that offered a lifestyle and culture that I believed I would enjoy potentially for the rest of my working life and thereafter. The short-term adjustment challenges would have long-term benefits in quality of life and career satisfaction, I gambled. Still, it was hard to pull the trigger and yank up stakes.

But the angst is counterbalanced by the excitement, renewal, opportunity and sense of adventure that comes with starting fresh in a new place. It's a chance to recharge batteries and create something from scratch, to expand my universe and experiences, to grow and learn and build confidence, to stretch beyond the known and test myself.

For me, with memories of pulling into my retired distant relatives' house in Longboat Key, Florida in the dark after a 20-hour journey to start a new life as a 22-year-old sportswriter still vivid in my mind, those affirmatives made it worth going back to the future.

On Being Alone:
An Unanticipated Thanksgiving

Thanksgiving 2017 -- I had moved into my new apartment in Summerville, SC just five days before Thanksgiving and two weeks into a new job, which I took to start a new career in counseling, more than 500 miles from where I had called "home" for nearly three decades, Maryland. It was too soon to fly back to see family for the holiday, and too ominous to face the Thanksgiving Day and subsequent weekend travel frenzies. Besides, my kids were scattered – my daughter in France for her post-college job teaching English and my son visiting his mother in Texas.

So I resigned myself to that most melancholia of situations that Americans seek desperately to avoid – spending a hyped holiday alone. I was too new in my adopted hometown to be taken in as a Thanksgiving orphan – barely anybody even knew I existed here, save for my new work colleagues and one college alum.

I was destined to join those invisible people who had nowhere to go for a holiday that screamed Americana, with its pilgrim, culinary, family, togetherness and football customs, and nobody coming to visit them – the stereotypical widowers, spinsters, shut-ins, homeless, outcasts, infirm, aged, black sheep, oddballs, cat ladies, mountain men, lone wolves, eccentrics, hermits, hoarders, rejects and recluses.

I searched for a volunteer opportunity to serve meals to the less fortunate on Thanksgiving Day, but couldn't find one. A big meal-serving charity in

Charleston already was overloaded with volunteers and could accept no more, and other organizations needed help in the days before Thanksgiving. I settled on volunteering for the Turkey Day Run 5K in Charleston, SC, a big fund-raising event. That got me out at 6 a.m. and occupied me on a chilly, rainy day until 10:30 a.m.

For the preceding week, a common salutation with clients at work, exchanged both ways, was "Have a good Thanksgiving," or, "So what are you doing for Thanksgiving?" constant reminders that I was doing nothing for Thanksgiving and that Thanksgiving, if I stayed strong mentally and emotionally, would be no worse than any other day, but certainly not "good" or "happy" in the traditional sense of celebrating a sacred time with friends and loved ones.

When I returned to my apartment, I did what anyone would do on a rainy day holiday with nowhere to go and nobody to entertain – took a long nap to sleep some of the day away.

If spending a uniquely American holiday alone was melancholy to begin with, it was amplified by my Spartan living conditions. I have no furniture – none. My place is bare, except for the air mattress serving as my bed, a food cooler as my chair and a plastic container as my dining table. I could not fit any furniture in my car for the move, and I won't be returning "home" to retrieve furniture and pack a rental truck for another two weeks. Not even a TV or a stereo or Internet. Silence. Just my books. On my Thanksgiving menu: catfish and frozen sweet potato fries.

When I awoke around 4, I decided to get out of my threadbare confines and bring my computer to the apartment complex's clubhouse, where I could get Internet connection and watch the football games. I predicted I would have the place to myself, as other residents would be celebrating Thanksgiving with friends and family elsewhere.

As I approached the clubhouse, I saw a bunch of people mingling inside.

"Oh, great. Booked for a private party," I thought. *"Looks like back to my apartment for catfish and a book."* But I decided to check to make sure.

"Is this a private party?" I asked the woman who greeted me at the door.

"No, come on in. We're The Misfits," she replied.

"Are you sure?" I asked, still feeling as though I was crashing a closed event. "I didn't bring anything."

"Don't worry about it. We've got plenty," she replied.

I entered to find about 40 people, from toddlers to grandparents, celebrating around a veritable Thanksgiving buffet feast. Turns out, The Misfits were what my greeter called "implants" – well, she meant "transplants," not people with dental work – people at the apartment complex and their friends who had moved to South Carolina from elsewhere and had no family nearby. They had been gathering for holidays and other events for several years.

I stayed for several hours, stuffing myself, watching football, and meeting friendly people in a festive environment. It sure beat being alone, and made for a surprising, grateful Thanksgiving.

That said, being alone is not dreadful. It does not equate to sadness, depression, or even necessarily loneliness. It's not to be feared. I often embrace solitude, and have done and continue to do many things by myself, even though I enjoy social activities, spending time with friends and being a family man. Enjoying solitary pursuits and engaging in social endeavors are not mutually exclusive. I'm an introvert. I am often more inspired by things I do alone than energized by being around lots of people. But that doesn't mean I don't like a good party or social outings.

Being alone is about being comfortable with the self, and knowing that it is a condition that one can change if desired. It is about finding things to do that one values and from which one derives pleasure when undertaken alone. It is about feeling worthy and valuable as a human being, even if one is alone, at least temporarily. It is about being comfortable turning inward and exploring the messages of one's own soul – the often hidden wants as well as the often elusive sense of peace and acceptance, the true self – rather than constantly craving and responding to external stimuli. It is about having the chance to slow down, quiet the mind, reflect and recharge, and direct one's energies toward passions, free from the pulls and distractions of others' wants, needs, expectations and demands.

By twist of fate, my 2017 Thanksgiving combined both ends of the spectrum – aloneness and togetherness. I give thanks for both in my life.

CHAPTER 3

Career: The Search for Meaning

YOLO: Don't Fear the
Late Career Change

Good news for "older" workers seeking to change their careers and find more fulfilling work comes from the American Institute for Economic Research in a new study, *New Careers for Older Workers*:

- ❖ Among workers ages 45-and-over who attempted a career change, 82 percent of late-in-career changers were considered successful.
- ❖ The majority of successful career changers said that the change made them happier.
- ❖ Many successful career changers saw an increase in income.
- ❖ Possessing transferable skills is one of the most important factors in determining the success of a career change.

The majority of late-in-career changers reported that their stress levels declined, it did not take too long to find a job, and that they felt they were following a passion. An obstacle was pay cuts, but career-changers reported that after a period of hard work and persistence, their incomes rose.

The study concludes that a career change later in life is "a viable choice" for those seeking work in an occupation that uses their current skills, and that one determinant of success is gaining a realistic view of what the transition will entail and preparing for it. While the study can't dispel the common perception that age discrimination in hiring exists, it does offer some evidence that some employers are open to hiring older workers.

I have changed careers twice before – from journalism to public relations, which isn't such a big leap, and a wholesale change to the battleground of inner-city teaching.

As the study referenced, the change from journalism to public relations involved transferable skills. My more dramatic career change to urban education was prompted by market conditions, the factor that influenced many career changers in the study. Consecutive public relations job layoffs motivated me to try a new career that I had contemplated before, and I entered a Baltimore teacher-training program for career-changers and non-educators. But I didn't last long in that field, bailed out and parachuted back to PR.

Now I'm halfway through a graduate program for counseling while continuing to work in PR. I am not sure where my program is going to lead, or if I will necessarily change careers again. It's a journey of faith, and I'm enjoying the process, the learning and the people. If I were to change careers ultimately, my income level would surely drop. But I also think there would be potential for my income to exceed my current level if I switched fields, with hard work, certain choices and passion, as the study indicated.

My program is full of potential career-changers in their 40s or older. In the class on Group Theory I just completed, there are two engineers – including one who is going to retire from his position in two months when he graduates and embark on a totally different career path. There's also an accountant, a nurse, a fashion designer, a financial professional, teachers and former military members. Every one of them seems happy and inspired that they are pursuing a new path. It's invigorating. The passion and investment of self is palpable. Some feel called to what they are pursuing; all seem to feel a sense of liberation to be pursuing their sense of vision for themselves. For many, it is a deeply spiritual quest.

So for anyone who thinks it's too late or that they have too much to lose or that a change would be doomed to failure and prove to be a big mistake, take a look at the results of this study that suggest otherwise.

And to feel a little younger at heart, consider the millennial, social media buzzword delivered by a student commencement speaker at my daughter's high school graduation: YOLO, as in "You Only Live Once."

Career Change at 50 'Can Be a Perilous Thing'

Altering a career course at fifty can be a perilous thing, and many people, if not most, do not traipse merrily down that path. The luckiest among us find their work fulfilling, and cannot imagine why they would leave. Others would follow their passions if they could, but college tuition, the mortgage, and the care of parents or children or both buckle them into their present work…Still others are simply scared – with good reason, because the job market does not necessarily embrace mid-career transitions.

Barbara Bradley Hagerty, Life Reimagined

I embarked on a path to a new career at 48. It was more like entering a maze – I couldn't see what was around the next corner, let alone envision arriving at the destination. I had doubts about whether I would have the fortitude to finish, and whether I actually even wanted to make a dramatic change and start over so late in my professional life.

I had established several decades of skills and experience as a journalist and public relations professional – fields that wouldn't earn me a cup of coffee in the new career I was pursuing. I wasn't just transferring and adjusting skills, as I did when I made the leap from journalism to PR. I was doing a total makeover, learning a new way of being.

"The brain likes its habits…and hates change," Bradley Hagerty quotes a Harvard Medical School professor. *"The brain despises conflict: It reasons that I may be happier over there, but I am earning a good paycheck here, and in general it resolves this cognitive dissonance in favor of the familiar. At the bottom of every dilemma is fear."*

To make the change I sought – becoming a mental health counselor/therapist – I had no choice but to return to school for a marathon master's degree venture, and ultimately confront the fear of the unfamiliar and the insecurity of the lower earnings commensurate with starting anew.

At first, I merely dipped my toe in the water by applying to a program and enrolling in the first of 22 required courses. I nearly dropped out after breaking my leg before completing my first course and losing motivation, feeling overwhelmed by the long road ahead. I overcame ambivalence and registered for a second course a few days before the next semester began. From there, it was a step-by-step progression that would have registered in the hundreds on a Fitbit.

After 5 ½ years of classes and internships and another five months of bureaucratic license- application process, I have been hired for my first professional job as a licensed counselor at age 54. As Bradley Hagerty writes in her book about midlife, it has not been a merry traipse, though it has been rewarding nonetheless – the sense of striving and accomplishment, the satisfaction of learning and growing, the excitement of pursuing something new and meaningful that will contribute toward others.

"The role of people in their second half of life is not to build up for themselves, but to begin to give away their time, energy and talents," Bradley Hagerty writes.

There have been costs accompanying the benefits. I left my job two years ago, largely because it was incompatible with the latter stages of the master's degree program, where I had to serve internships for four semesters. That plunged me from making a comfortable living to pay for a mortgage, two college tuitions and care of children – just as Bradley Hagerty identified – to an itinerant work life in the Gig Economy, working lower-paying temporary, part-time and seasonal jobs. Breaking even on the monthly household budget, much less saving for retirement, went out the window.

Psychologically and emotionally, I felt unmoored. After all, what kind of responsible, mature man in his 50s would be working the same summer job alongside college students as a tennis teacher? Wasn't I supposed to be at the peak of my earning power – indeed, the job I left provided me the highest salary I had ever made – instead of making the same hourly wages I earned in my 20s? All this so I could enter a new career at the bottom rung in a profession where beginning pay is notoriously low. Just to drive home the point that I'm a rookie, my license for my first two years identifies me as "Licensed Professional Counselor-***Intern***."

Was I scared, as Bradley Hagerty suggests many midlife career deliberators rightly are, *"because the job market does not necessarily embrace mid-career transitions?"*

No…at least not so much to be deterred. I was more scared about looking back in a decade still with a yearning to try something new and realizing with regret that I missed my window. Once midlife careens on the backside toward older age, it becomes even harder to reinvent the self.

I also was entering a job market where there is a growing need, where men are relatively scarce and therefore actually valued for their gender perspective and traits, and where the accumulation of life experience and wisdom that comes with age is an advantage in helping other people with their problems – unlike some other professions, where older workers become dinosaurs because they can't keep up with technology, trends, new methods and the requisite energy to stay on top. Or they are paid at the high end of the salary range, making them expendable in favor of hungry and more footloose up-and-comers.

Altering a career course at 50 certainly can be a perilous thing. There's no guarantee the job market will unfurl a welcome mat for a midlife career changer or that the changer will be successful, however success is measured. I've managed to get through the front door; now I'll find out for myself whether the new house I'm entering truly is my dream home.

15 Principles for Surviving and Executing a Career Transition

March 2017 -- In two months I will complete a graduate degree in clinical mental health counseling that will have taken 5½ years to finish, enabling me to take final steps to executing a fairly drastic midlife career change from public relations. I had made a career change before, from journalism to public relations. Though still jarring, that transition was significantly more seamless than this one, requiring no additional education and using many of the same skills.

I have been seeking to derive more meaning and satisfaction from my career, as well as the opportunity to self-direct my future, embrace an entrepreneurial spirit, contribute value to society and work flexibly, creatively, collaboratively and independently. I explored life-coaching, completing a series of training courses, but ultimately didn't pursue it. But the idea of helping people with psychological, emotional and life challenges stuck with me.

It took me about three years of mulling the idea to apply to graduate school for counseling and another year after acceptance to enroll in my first class. Twenty-one classes and three internships later, I'm on the precipice of a career transition.

It hasn't been easy. As I started my internships, I ran into a buzz saw at my PR job. It was miserable, and at the same time the best thing that could have happened. I couldn't have done both twell simultaneously, along with graduate classes. I would have burned out. I left my job, and the security blanket of a biweekly paycheck.

That was 18 months ago. Since then, I've lived a much more itinerant, unpredictable and frugal existence, cobbling together temporary, seasonal and part-time jobs, and unpaid or low-paid internships. In brief, these are 15 principles I've learned about making a significant career change, concepts that are valuable to consider while mulling a change or while bulldozing through the trenches:

1. **Long-Term Vision** – A career transition won't happen if you can't envision a different future, if you are too overwhelmed by the daily grind and stressors to dream about a new life.
2. **Delay Gratification/Patience** – Depending on how drastic the change and the amount of education and training required, the transition could be a long haul rather than a quick fix.
3. **Risk (Tolerance/Acceptance)** – You will be giving up something known for something new, with no guarantee of breaking in, or even being proficient at or liking the new endeavor.
4. **Self-Knowledge** – Become clear on what is most important to you, your values, how much risk you can tolerate, and how hard you are willing to work to make a change happen.
5. **Courage** – You'll have to be brave enough to take risks and step out of your comfort zone.
6. **Confidence/Self-Assuredness** – Consider how you will handle other people in your life, including those closest to you and colleagues in

your current occupation, questioning or casting aspersions on your decisions. How much would a wave of skepticism and criticism deter you or affect your thinking and beliefs?

7. **Identity** – Leaving a profession, especially one you've worked at for years and in which you've achieved a certain level of expertise, status and success, can significantly alter how you identify yourself. Can your ego withstand such an identity loss, while building a new and different piece of your identity?

8. **Research/Network** – It will be important to determine the costs and requirements (and barriers) to entry into a new profession, as well as occupational outlook, such as job growth and salary projections. Soak up all the information you can about your prospective new career while considering a transition and in the transitional phase by interviewing people in the field, networking with fellow career changers and professors, taking classes, attending conferences and reading industry journals.

9. **Commitment/Persistence** – A half-hearted or uncertain effort will likely fail to result in lasting change, like my foray into coaching. The urge to give up may hit, especially early in the process. You'll have to constantly re-evaluate your commitment, revisit why you embarked on the effort in the first place and resist inevitable doubts.

10. **Embrace Uncertainty/Unpredictability –** Become comfortable with not knowing and embracing the journey as an adventure. View unpredictability as making life more exciting, stimulating and challenging. Here's where **faith** and **spirituality** can come into play.

11. **Sacrifice –** Be prepared to pay costs in terms of money, time, effort, perceived security and status (you may go from being expert to novice).

12. **Hustle/Scramble/Diversify –** A career transition may not be seamless, moving directly from a job in one career to a job in another. There may be an intermediary period involving education, training, internships and the like. You may have to jump off the cliff during this period – leaving security behind – but with a parachute. You just won't be able to be sure where you may drift or land along the way. You may have to be aggressive in patching together a living from various jobs that aren't career jobs, but serve as a means to your end. You may have to call on skills you weren't using in your current career, or adapt your skills to different positions that work within your new goals. For me, that meant working summers as a tennis teacher and applying writing and teaching skills as a university writing tutor.

13. **Flexibility –** A flexible frame of mind complements the principles of identity and hustle. If you are not rigid in your identity, you

can explore varied employment opportunities, living arrangements and lifestyles that can help you manage the transition. If you are open to a wide range of income-producing opportunities, you can minimize your reluctance to try new things – perhaps jobs you would have once considered beneath you -- and ramp up your hustle to get them.

14.   **Financial House** – Your transition will be easier and less stressful if there is Order in the House, the Financial House. As much and as far ahead as possible, craft a financial plan for the transition. Build savings cushions and tuition accounts, if education is necessary. Consider becoming a minimalist in your lifestyle choices. A transition likely will come with some financial pain, including possibly a precipitous income drop from your previous career once you start in a new occupation, but planning and frugality can mitigate the potential pitfalls.

15.   **Negotiation** – If you're lucky, you'll have a current employer who respects, or maybe even encourages and supports, your career-change endeavor (I wasn't). If so, see how you can negotiate to get what you need – time, a flexible schedule, tuition assistance, remote work arrangement – while continuing to fulfill your employer's needs. You may be able to hold onto your job and income much longer (I couldn't), helping to bridge the transition.

Joining the Gig Economy

I am a member of the Gig Economy.

I didn't plan to join. It just evolved.

Giggers don't count. We're under the radar. The U.S. Bureau of Labor can't find us for all its employment reports. We're a step above underground. We exist in the netherworld between employed and unemployed, worker and slacker. Above all, we are free agents, with shallow allegiances, if any.

Nothing is secure. Nothing is long-term. Nothing is permanent. But then again, that applies to most traditional jobs nowadays, except for government employment. Those who convince themselves otherwise are fooling themselves.

If I don't work, I don't get paid. In my circumstance, sometimes even when I do work, I don't get paid. There are no benefits – except the ability to say "yes" or "no" to anything, and to make your own choices, agreements and schedule. No paid vacation, no sick leave, no retirement savings programs, no health or life insurance. Not even any guarantee of hours or certain amount of pay per week – or free coffee.

Income is unpredictable. One thing that is predictable is that Giggers will constantly be scrambling for income, replacing one lost or concluded gig with another.

An October 13, 2016 CNBC report said employment in the Gig Economy is growing "far faster" than traditional payroll employment, according to a Brookings Institution study. An author of the report said the data showed a trend indicating a "potentially seismic reorganization" of the economy and employment arrangements.

Until a year ago, I counted. I was included in the Labor category "Employed." For the previous 10 years, I held two traditional jobs, with a salary and benefits. As long as I showed up each day, I could get paid the same, whether I surfed the Internet all day and took two-hour lunches or hunkered down and grinded on the corporation's mission. Not anymore.

At the same time I began the two-year internship portion of my interminable master's degree program in counseling – a minimum 15-to-20 hour weekly commitment – my full-time public relations job started going south because of institutional disarray. My employer and I soon ended our union. I was suddenly without the safety net of the full-time, permanent gig, except for the frayed, patchwork, hole-ridden net of the Gig Economy.

I sought a flexible, low-key part-time job to make money and work around my counseling internship. I quickly got a call back from a young company which contracted with day care centers, pre-schools and other schools using the game of soccer to educate and coach kids through an activity- and fun-based curriculum. I visited a pre-school three times to observe and assist one of the company's trainers teach an interactive lesson with the 15 kids, and then to execute lessons from the curriculum myself. In the end, I got an ego blow. I was rejected with no explanation; I can only imagine my sweet spot wasn't in managing and engaging 3-year-olds. Perhaps I was too old, out of my element; my trainer was all of 23. Welcome to the Gig Economy! But this gig ain't for you! Go find another.

Eventually, I fell back on teaching tennis on weekends, an income-producing gig I had relied upon during other periods of unemployment, and ramped up my hours as a counseling intern at an outpatient mental health center, something that was impossible to do while working full-time and which significantly aided me in meeting my master's degree requirements. But my income was in the toilet.

I landed a great gig for the summer, between academic semesters and internships, as a tennis teacher at a resort in Bethany Beach, DE. But like many gigs, it was short-term, offered no benefits, and produced an unpredictable income stream.

For the time I taught on court, I made decent money. If I wasn't teaching – waiting around at the club for the next paying hour or bumped out of teaching because of too little customer demand and my low ranking on the pecking order of tennis pros – I made minimum wage. I taught a good amount over the summer – but also spent much time earning $8.25 per hour. The job ran parallel with vacation season, late May to Labor Day.

At 4 p.m. on Labor Day, the gig was up and my income ceased. Now I'm cobbling together an income from three sources – another counseling internship, where I'm lucky I get paid at all, but only at half-rate and only when erratic and inconsistent clients show up; a writing tutor job at Loyola University, where I'm a student; and itinerant tennis teaching. I'm working erratic hours seven days a week. And I'm still searching for more work – more regular and consistent tennis teaching to maximize income for my still-available, Swiss-cheese hours.

The nature of membership in the Gig Economy is to be in a constant state of searching and scrambling for the next gig, the most reliable gig, the best-paying gig for the time we must devote to it. We can't rest, lest the hour glass runs out. We have to see beyond the horizon, because everything ends or fizzles out. We have to be chess players, thinking three or four moves ahead.

But membership in the Gig Economy has its advantages. I'm much happier with my work than I was at my last job. I have flexibility and control over my schedule. I have variety. I'm not bored at anything I do. I can move on when I feel like it with little angst. I like the direction I'm moving. I'm more free and self-directed.

I may hold other permanent jobs in the future, likely in a counseling capacity. But I'm also pretty certain I will be retaining membership in the Gig Economy for the rest of my working life in one form or another. It's just a matter of putting all the necessary pieces together. I am a free agent, and I like it that way.

Sweating it out to the End

I was sitting in the sauna after a swim, trying to meditate (and lose a pound), when the thought hit me (a welcome thought, nevertheless showing I don't know how to meditate): the only thing separating me from graduation with a clinical mental health counseling master's degree was one more paper, the fourth chapter of a final project.

In the heat, I felt a surge of accomplishment, the dripping sweat an appropriate metaphor for the 5 ½-year graduate school and internship marathon. I reflected on all that had happened during that time – a broken leg requiring surgery and a year of recovery; turning 50; my mother dying; leaving a seven-year job under contentious and demoralizing circumstances; both of my kids leaving for college – and felt amazed I had arrived at this moment. I had nearly dropped out after the first of my 22 classes and three internships, the path seemed so complicated and daunting.

So other than giving myself a pat on the back for perseverance, what can my experience say about sweating it out for a goal at midlife that perhaps could resonate with others?

- ❖ Personal growth and development keeps life interesting. I feel more alive and engaged with new challenges and goals to pursue, and restless when I feel stagnated and mired in routine.
- ❖ It's never too late to learn new things or set new goals. Changing careers is another matter entirely

that involves issues of practicality, responsibility, risk and sacrifice. But these complexities shouldn't preclude exploration.

❖ Moving forward on faith can work out, and could be a necessity for progress. Sometimes pushing through doubts is the only way forward. I still don't know how my whole counseling endeavor ultimately will work out, but I have faith that it will. Needing a guarantee on an outcome may preclude the journey.

❖ Find a way. Don't let something that seems too hard stop you, if you can creatively discover ways to make it work, even just one step at a time, especially if you believe you might live with regret for giving up on a goal or dream too easily. I feared living with regret, which helped propel me to continue grinding ahead. Sometimes "a way" may seem impossible, but perhaps as likely self-imposed limits make it seem so.

❖ Pursuing something new, whether a hobby, pastime, education or career, can bring you into contact with a new community that can enrich your life. The people I've met through my graduate program have provided community, enhancing my life and helping me learn.

I'm sure hoping this new counseling gig works out. I entered the Loyola University-Maryland Pastoral Counseling program at age 48. Back then, I couldn't imagine getting to the end, which has now arrived at age 54. I'm excited to see where it leads. At the least, it will open up a whole new range of opportunities and a greater chance to self-direct my career – possibly in the form of my own business and other entrepreneurial endeavors – as I head into its latter stages. I'm feeling now all the sweat I've poured into it has been worthwhile.

Do the Limbo. Or, How to Be 'Comfortable with Ambiguity.'

I am in limbo. Complete and utter limbo.

However, the bar is not set low and I am not trying to shimmy under. The bar is high and I am aspiring to clear it like a Fosbury Flop, a la Dick Fosbury, the first backward-flopping high-jumper.

It's not supposed to be like this as a 54-year-old, according to societal expectations. I'm supposed to be settled, stable, predictable, a rock, boring in my steadiness. I chose another path, paved with uncertainty. It's come with a loss of income, stability and predictability. But I expect the payoff will come in the form of greater life and career satisfaction, and income growth ultimately will follow as I hopefully find passion in my work.

My limbo status is largely of my own design and in small part due to the bugaboo of bureaucracy.

I have 11 days left until my second summer teaching tennis at the Sea Colony resort in Bethany Beach, DE runs out on Labor Day and I return home, jobless and anxious but optimistic.

I have spent nearly two years in the Gig Economy, ever since a non-amicable parting with a former employer allowed me to place more focus on a master's degree program in clinical mental health counseling and the two years of internships required to complete it, as part of a midlife career transition from public relations to counseling. I have been scrambling to piece together part-time, temporary and contractual jobs since I dropped out of the routine 9-to-5 world.

I graduated in May 2017, and expected that tennis teaching for 3 ½ months would provide the perfect bridge to the new career, allowing enough time for me to obtain the state license I need to be eligible to practice, get hired and begin work. But bureaucracy has brought that plan to a grinding halt, possibly leading me to the unemployment office rather than a counseling office, at least temporarily.

A long waiting period to get access to my "official verified" National Counselor Exam report has left my state license applications – and thus job prospects – in limbo, even though I have already been notified that I passed the exam. The blood pressure ticked a little higher each day over the last six weeks as I awaited an email notification from the national counselor certification body that my school transcript met all requirements, along with my exam score, for certification.

One former boss wrote in my annual performance review that I needed to be "comfortable with ambiguity." That was corporate speak for an organization refusing to accept accountability for its disorganization, poor leadership and incoherent, vacillating strategy. Ironically, now that I've left that organization, the advice applies.

My immediate future is ambiguous. I don't know where I'll be working as a counselor, or when. I don't know how long it will take state licensing boards to review my applications and grant a license. I don't even know what state I will be living in, as I have applied for license in Maryland and South Carolina.

So, what have I learned about being "comfortable with ambiguity?"

- ❖ Take things one day at a time, as cliché as that may sound. Thinking too much about unknowns in the future produces excessive worry but no solutions.
- ❖ Pursue aggressive actions whenever possible to address things over which you do have control, such as making networking contacts, applying to jobs and following up on leads. Taking action tends to boost motivation, confidence and attitude.
- ❖ Detach from the cell phone and computer for periods of time. It's tempting when living with job and income uncertainty to obsessively check for email and phone contacts, which increases anxiety each time none have come through.
- ❖ Have faith that putting what you want to attract into the universe ultimately will materialize for you, with persistence, patience and a positive outlook.
- ❖ Continue doing things you like to do (that are free or low-cost) to keep your spirits high and take your mind off worries.
- ❖ Squirrel away your nuts (money). Live cheaply (the Minimalist lifestyle) while dealing with ambiguity, to reduce financial pressures.

Limbo is not a comfortable place to be when you have financial and family obligations, when you feel like you should be occupying a certain status and you're not, and when you like to plan and predict your life with a high degree of certainty. But for me, my current state of limbo is a necessary part of the process of getting where I want to be, just another stage of the journey, another bar to traverse.

A Different Perch for the Schoolyard Bully: The Boss's Seat

You would think this would be an enlightened era in the arena of workplace conduct, civility and respect, with increased awareness of women's and minority rights, civil rights, equal opportunity, discrimination, sexual and other forms of harassment, and generally boorish behavior.

Yet workplace bullying appears to be pervasive and an expanding style and strategy of management, with little or no repercussions for the perpetrators, who use this style to enhance their power and intimidate, victimize, marginalize, humiliate and deflate their subordinates. Or in some cases, it's a tactic used by peers to assert dominance and solidify position in the pecking order.

Management, including human resources departments, often has more interest in protecting the bully, who may be perceived as productive, effective and a company loyalist. The victim of the bully may be viewed as a whiner or troublemaker, and doubted and even blamed. Bullying in the workplace is not illegal, and any legal remedies for discrimination or hostile work environment can be time-consuming, costly, stressful, hard to prove and difficult to achieve.

It is not just the young, inept or the weak who are victims. In fact, skilled, seasoned, accomplished, competent and productive workers – many who are in midlife and at a time they should be thriving professionally – are the most likely to experience bullying at work. Chances are, you'll experience bullying from a superior during your worklife.

In my career, workplace bullying has been alive and well in work environments. I've been bullied, and fought back with everything I had in my arsenal, including union, contractual and legal remedies.

In one job at a health care nonprofit, a complaint about pervasive bullying as a management style by supervisors was expressed clearly and anonymously by employees in a survey, to the surprise and apparent dismay of top management. You would think a health care organization would embody the values of caring, dignity, respect and fair treatment, but it was not immune from bullying behavior.

Bullying can thrive in any work environment, not just in testosterone-stoked, competitive industries, especially if management is oblivious, willfully ignores – or even worse, insidiously defends or condones -- such conduct.

My employer had no policy or system in place to address bullying behavior. The stopgap remedy? Make a complaint to the organization's compliance officer, the corporate attorney, whose main job was to protect management and the organization. Would you think that would engender confidence in an employee that their concern would be taken seriously and that they would have a fair chance at redress?

I'm no expert on workplace bullying. The Workplace Bullying Institute is. WBI defines workplace bullying as "repeated, health-harming mistreatment" and abusive conduct that is threatening, humiliating, or intimidating; verbally abusive; or which sabotages, or interferes with or prevents work from getting done. Bullying is driven by a perpetrator who feels compelled to control the targeted individual, and who chooses targets, timing, location, and methods to inflict emotional abuse. Bullying behavior can be acts of commission or omission.

WBI has surveyed workers and studied the targets, causes, effects and prevalence of workplace bullying. The Institute's 2014 survey showed that more than 1 of 4 workers had current or past direct experience with abusive conduct at work.

WBI cautions workers about being overly reliant on their HR department to provide support and relief; HR's main function may be to buttress management and maintain status quo.

WBI has found that likely targets of workplace bullying are:

- ❖ A "threat" to the perpetrator.
- ❖ Independent and refuse to be subservient. In reaction, bullies escalate their campaigns of intimidation to wrest control of the target's work.
- ❖ More technically skilled. Insecure bosses don't like to share credit, and steal credit from targets.
- ❖ Better liked, have more social skills, and may possess greater emotional intelligence. Others appreciate the warmth that the targets bring to the workplace.
- ❖ Ethical and honest. The most easily exploited targets exhibit a desire to help, heal, teach, develop, and nurture others.

❖ Not likely to confront, or respond to aggression with aggression. They pay the price in that the bully can act with impunity if the employer is unaware or does nothing in response.

❖ Likely to suffer stress-related health problems (nearly half, according to the 2007 WBI-Zogby Survey).

The loser in workplace bullying scenarios is far more likely to be the target than the perpetrator, according to a 2014 WBI survey. In 61 percent of cases, the target quit or lost his job, compared to 15 percent for the perpetrator.

If you are being bullied at work, you should know you are not alone. Then again, as research shows, the discouraging truth is that you may likely have a lonely battle on your hands to do anything constructive about it other than leaving your job or sucking it up and dealing, with all the attendant potential consequences to your health.

CHAPTER 4

Money

Good Money

When I would tell people I got a new job to start a new career in another state and would be moving, one of the first questions they'd inevitably ask was, "How much will you be making?" Or, so as to be less crass, "Will you be making **good money**?"

In our competitive, capitalist, consumerist society, it is only natural that money is the first thing that comes to mind when someone accepts a new position. To be sure, why would anyone choose to move more than 500 miles and three states away for a job if not to make **good money**?

I had three answers for that question, and all had validity:

1. Yes, of course I would be making **good money**, because there's no such thing as **bad money**.
2. No, I wouldn't be making **good money**, compared to the much **better money** I had made in previous jobs.
3. None of your friggin' business what kind of money!

The answer is not simple. My job as a therapist under a two-year provisional license pays considerably less than my previous positions in public relations. I am at the entry level in the mental health field, where salaries and pay, though variable depending upon many factors, are relatively low compared to many other professions.

However, my job pays considerably more annually than the series of Gig Economy counseling internships and part-time and temporary jobs I had pieced together for the final two years of my counseling master's degree program after leaving my full-time job. So viewed from that perspective, my new job does pay **good money**, and I'm grateful for that.

In midlife, we evaluate what we've already done and what we'd like to do with our remaining years, which no longer seem infinite. Priorities change, as we shift from the achievement-oriented, ladder-climbing, self-focused goals of younger adulthood to an increased desire to make a contribution to others, pursue meaningful activities and leave a legacy. My change to a career in counseling reflects the internal re-evaluations of the midlife transitional period.

When you realign priorities and make a significant change, there will be sacrifices. For me, one of those was money – **good money**. I knew that consequence of my decision from the start, when I embarked on the graduate program nearly six years before actually entering the counseling field. But I ignored that inescapable fact at the time.

Now that my new level of pay is a reality, I'm adjusting my life and budget to match. I may not yet qualify as a full-fledged Minimalist, but I've moved closer to that end of the scale in my spending, decision-making and thinking.

I don't want to minimize the importance of making money – ***good money*** – or pretend I don't care. It certainly helps in many ways and I always endeavored to make ***good money*** – at least the best I could in any given circumstance. I'd certainly rather be well-off and feel secure than poor and living anxiously paycheck to paycheck. Wouldn't everyone? Fortunately, I have some financial cushion, enough to allow me to overcome the financial anxieties of making a career change, but far below some golden threshold to claim money doesn't really matter.

But making ever more ***good money*** – however one defines it -- isn't the end-all be-all path to an ever more glorious Shangri-La, as a 2010 Princeton University study concluded. The Princeton researchers found that no matter how much more than $75,000 per year that a person earned, their "degree of happiness," or emotional well-being did not increase. It also found that, though earning less than $75,000 in and of itself did not cause people to feel more unhappy, it did magnify and intensify negative feelings from life problems they had.

Beyond the practical realities of how I spend and the reduced margin of discretionary money available to save or burn compared to my previous work life, I've had to make a humbling mental adjustment: Here I am, in my 50s, peak earning years, with two graduate degrees, making less than half of what I made at my last full-time job, and less than or equivalent to many workers with much less education or years of experience than I have. Yet, I would still contend I am making **good money,** not **bad money**.

I gain fulfillment and a sense of purpose and contribution from counseling people and helping them improve their lives. Work is stimulating, rewarding and challenging, which I couldn't always claim before. I look forward to my future in this new profession, and its many opportunities for learning, growth and entrepreneurship.

For those reasons, I know I can take this to the bank: I *am* making **good money**, with the promise of **better money** to come. When you truly enjoy what you are doing for a living and apply yourself with a passion because of that, the money naturally tends to follow. **Good money**.

Living on the Cheap

Since I left my full-time, public relations job in October 2015 to focus on my unpaid counseling internship and a full-time course load as a master's degree candidate in pastoral counseling, I've adapted to living on the cheap.

I can't say I'm living a deprived life or even struggling. I have everything I need and much more. I can't say I have any idea what it's like to live day-to-day, hand-to-mouth, wondering where the next meal will come from or worrying about losing my shelter. Comparatively, I'm well-off, not one of the "1 percenters" but probably closer to that than the bottom 75 percent.

But I am more aware of, and closely monitoring, my discretionary spending, much more than when I knew my bank account would be replenished with an equal amount every two weeks. I am subscribing to minimalism, at least to some extent, as described in the book, *Everything That Remains* by The Minimalists.

Still, just as I'm transitioning careers in midlife, I've hit a time of financial stress and challenges.

In addition to my own graduate school tuition, I'll have two children in college in the fall. Three simultaneous higher educations will blast a cannonball-sized hole in any family budget. I am not so many years away from typical retirement age – though with my new career, I plan to work as long as I want and don't ever envision really retiring. And if the theory holds true that you will need $1 million in retirement to last, I have a long way to go. And I have an aging parent who could need financial help in the future.

Despite my income needs, I reached a point where I knew I couldn't adeptly handle a full-time job, a part-time internship and graduate school classes, and perform any of them well and with full focus, without suffering from stress, exhaustion and dissatisfaction. Trying to handle them all might have doomed completion of the counseling master's degree after a four-year investment.

Luckily, I have a wife with stable employment (though with a company known for frequent layoffs and restructurings) that has provided a financial anchor while I scramble to produce more erratic income from various sources.

That's what brought me to the Sea Colony Tennis resort in Bethany Beach, DE to work as a seasonal tennis instructor for the summer. Though it required me to be away from home, it provided the greatest earning potential for the short period between internships and semesters.

I found the cheapest place I could rent, no easy feat along the shore – that's why I'm living three miles away from the beach. I'm living with two roommates. One roommate is another tennis instructor who is living similarly frugally. He turned me on to the Dollar Store, where we've bought a lot of our food, toiletries, medications and household items at half the cost of the grocery store. We found the Atlantic Community Thrift Store, where I got a cool Old Navy bathing suit for $2 and he found a Pinehurst Golf jacket for pennies on the dollar and a desk chair for $3. My roommate has found a way to play several holes of golf for free by walking onto a course near our house after regular hours.

I've been here for 15 days, and have gone out for a meal only once, my first night. It's tempting, with all the restaurants, seafood and pizza joints and junk food establishments at the beach, but I've held off so far. I question each expense to determine if it's necessary, while still allowing certain indulgences like Dollar Store sale-priced Doritos and ice cream bars.

The tennis teaching season has started relatively slow, while school is still in session and most tennis-player vacations are planned for July and August. That's when I'll make my money and the investment to live away from home pay off.   I'm conscious that going out for a beer and appetizer plus tip can wipe out the earnings of a one-hour tennis clinic, and what would be the point of that?

My one other indulgence was the clunky, antique, heavy-as-hell cash register I bought on a whim on my way to move to the beach at a roadside antique and junk shop. Even then, I bargained the proprietor down from $50 to $20. I have no idea its worth and it needs some refurbishing, but it looks retro-stylish. I think the guy just wanted to get rid of it, an indication it's not worth much in its worn condition.

Living cheaply means living more simply. I like it. As long as I have enough income to meet my needs and preferably a few wants, I'm happy. It's less stressful than trying to always make more money so I can live bigger, have more and maintain more. Living cheaply, I can focus on the things that matter in life – connecting with people, improving relationships, pursuing fulfilling work, helping others and doing things I enjoy with my time, which will be more possible when my income needs are less.

Living on the cheap was brought about for me largely by necessity. But it is a lifestyle choice that I embrace.

Social Insecurity

God help me if, in my supposed "Golden Years," I'm hanging out by my mailbox, hopefully not hunched over like Quasimodo or leaning on a walker or sitting on a scooter (no offense to those who need them for mobility, I just hope it's not me), on a certain day of each month anxiously awaiting my Social Security check so I can survive for another month.

Often through no fault of their own – or sometimes, through bad luck, setbacks, unfortunate decisions, costly medical problems, lack of foresight and typical life struggles – that is the fate of many older people in the U.S. The fear that I may join them drives me to try to maximize my income-producing options for the future and save and invest as much as possible, as hard as it is with two college-age children, my own graduate school education, a mortgage, and a life in a metro area with one of the nation's highest costs of living.

The AARP's Retirement Confidence Survey revealed that nearly half of 50+ workers and nearly three in five retirees have less than $25,000 in savings and investments. That, to me, certainly seems like a crisis of poverty engulfing our elderly citizens.

Think about it: three of five retirees who may live 20 years in retirement may have $1,000 or less in savings and investments for each of those years. That's a retirement of mere survival.

The survey found that Social Security is a major source of retirement income for two of three retirees over age 50.

The survey concluded that Americans age 50 and older may not have a realistic view of their financial future in retirement and are not adequately preparing for it.

Whether many people could possibly adequately prepare for it in this age is another matter, with wages and income stagnant in perpetuity; rampant employer layoffs, persistent and widespread unemployment and jobs shipped overseas; escalating and unaffordable college tuition; high student and consumer debt loads; and rising consumer costs and government fees and taxes.

In my state, Maryland, politicians are trying to force workers to save for retirement. A new legislative effort was launched to establish retirement security plans for more than a million Marylanders who would otherwise rely entirely on Social Security in retirement.

U.S. Labor Secretary Tom Perez joined Maryland leaders to promote the national initiative at the state level: the creation of workplace savings accounts in which employees would be automatically enrolled but would have the right to bow out of participation.

While I believe the financial fate of the nation's elderly is important to the U.S. economy and society's overall health and well-being, I contend that the government is overstepping its reach in this effort of forced "workplace savings accounts." I also believe in individual responsibility and accountability and free choice. And where does this policy leave entrepreneurs, consultants and other non-traditional income earners in this unstable economy which is increasingly moving toward a free-agent model and employers cannot be counted upon for a secure job for life?

As for me, this fear of over-reliance on somewhat meager Social Security payments is one of my motivations for pursuing a graduate degree in mental health counseling. Counseling is something I can do independently to produce income if I so choose, and a career that doesn't necessarily come with a built-in retirement date. It expands my options, and I want all the options I can generate at my disposal to live life on my own terms in the future.

A Full Pension but Half a Life?
Your Money or Your Time

What is of more value to you: Your money or your time?

I had an interesting, offhand discussion about this with a classmate in my counseling graduate program. She is in the engineering field, working for a power company, is probably in her mid- to late-50s, and has three grown children. So she is aiming to be a career-changer later in life, similar to my path, going from journalism to public relations to counseling.

The difference between us is that, after grinding through the counseling program at a slow pace for four years, I am now trying to make a stronger commitment to serving my internships, completing my degree and making the transition. My classmate, also proceeding slowly at one course per semester, said she is considering working for five more years at her company so she can get a full pension instead of two-thirds or more of the pension's value if she leaves sooner.

We talked only briefly, but since we are in a counseling program, we are accustomed to talking about life issues that really matter. Essentially, I asked her whether, if counseling truly was a passion for her, was it worth trading five more years of her life doing something she was not passionate about to have a somewhat higher income in retirement or old age? Or could she figure out how to make do with a smaller pension as a tradeoff for making a complete transition sooner and bringing more joy and inspiration to her life?

She studied my line of questioning for a moment and seemed to re-evaluate her priorities. She offered that she knew a man at her company who stayed long enough to collect a full pension. Problem was, within a year of retiring, he died. None of us know how much time we have. It would seem a shame to have a full pension but half a life.

In the few moments we had before class, I suggested an option that might reduce my classmates' perceived need for a larger pension: minimalism. I had just read a book, *Everything That Remains*, by Joshua Fields Millburn, espousing the benefits of living a minimalist life.

Essentially, that means getting rid of everything that in your life that does not have real value, does not improve your life and is not needed, which could mean material possessions, unnecessary living space, services, relationships, jobs and other things we imagine we cannot live without, when we really can, and better.

Instead of arranging your finances to fit your lifestyle – the one you think you need – you imagine and create the lifestyle that will make you happy, and adapt your finances to fit that.

How many of us could live a downscaled lifestyle and fill it with things that really make us happy and inspired, if we only really examined what that would mean and took actions to make it happen? How many of us live with more stress and anxiety because of all the things we need to maintain and hold onto even when we don't really want them, much of the time out of fear, and then compound the stress by feeling the need to make enough money to maintain the things that don't really make us happy and free?

I don't know what my classmate will decide to do. But I'm at the point in my life where I would gladly exchange some degree of financial security for the risk and reward of pursuing a passion – or at least something close to it – and creating a life that I can truly say that I want, not one I feel obligated to soldier through out of some sense of being secure or safe, or doing what I believe society expects me to do.

Divorced Parents with United Financial Goals

One of the toughest things about divorce is untangling and dividing finances, and planning and making financial agreements for the future that each party can live up to when kids are involved. Fortunately, my ex-wife and I have done a pretty good job at that, and it's paying off now.

Money battles between divorced parents and short-sightedness not only cause intense acrimony between the former husband and wife, but almost unavoidably will spill over into relationships between the parents and the kids and cause more turmoil, stress and anxiety. Challenging enough that parents who once combined incomes to create more buying power and economies of scale have to double down on everything after divorce – housing, property taxes, furniture, electricity, cable, maintenance costs, health and car insurance and more – without negatively affecting relationships and kids' attitudes, perceptions and sense of well-being and security.

My ex-wife and I are likely going through our greatest time of financial stress since our separation 11 years ago right now, yet we are weathering it well (I can't be positive, but I think I can speak for both of us).

In fall 2016, both our children will be in college at the same time. In addition, I am in a graduate school program for counseling, so I'll be paying for three higher education degrees simultaneously.

But a few things have saved us from potentially extreme financial pressures and enormous debt. First, we planned for the kids' college education early in their lives, investing in Maryland's prepaid college tuition program (for two years' tuition) when they were 4 and 2. We also opened Education IRAs for each child around the same time. Second, when we divorced, we agreed to continue contributing to each fund on an arranged schedule, and each of us adhered to the agreement. Third, I opened Maryland 529 college investment accounts for me and both kids a few years before my oldest entered college to help fund my education and fill in inevitable gaps in theirs. Finally, each kid made wise choices to attend state universities, where tuition costs are half or less of private or out-of-state colleges.

My ex-wife and I each have had the discipline, cooperation and foresight to keep contributing to the kids' college educations, even though we were no longer united or in agreement on other things. Sending both kids to college still will make a big dent in my monthly budget and annual cash flow.

But as a result of our advanced planning and divorce agreements, I believe each kid will be able to graduate from college debt-free (and me from my graduate program without wiping out savings and investments). That will be a huge gift to each of them, and a big benefit in starting out their adult lives.

Working together with an ex-spouse after a divorce, as aggravating and imperfect as it may be at times, certainly pays off, both for the kids and the adults going their own ways.

Debt: The Mosquito in my Ear

Debt nags me like a mosquito buzzing my ear as I try to sleep.

I've spent my midlife trying to get out of debt while preserving assets – in other words, reducing debt with current income while attempting to avoid incurring more liabilities or depleting investments. Sometimes I have had to unload investments to pay off debts, and always feel bad about it, like I'm filling a city street pothole that is sure to crater again.

Overall, I've been fairly successful at paying down and staving off debt. Still, whenever I become completely debt-free, something seems to suck me back "into the red" – a job loss, a major repair, education costs, or simply operating a budget that gets out of whack and spending beyond current means, a cash flow problem. I'm not alone.

Americans are swimming in debt:

❖ The average American household that carries credit card debt has a balance of more than $15,000 on the cards, according to a 2017 NerdWallet survey. The same study found that the average American household carrying student loan debt owed $46,597 in education expenses, and the average American household with auto loans owed $27,669 for their vehicles.

❖ A 2014 Urban Institute study found that 35 percent of Americans with credit files had delinquent debt. That debt typically came from credit cards or medical or utility bills that was more than 180 days past due and had been turned over to collections. The debts averaged more than $5,000.

❖ In 2013, 7 out of 10 graduating college seniors were entering post-college life with student loans, which averaged $28,400, according to the Project on Student Debt.

Debt limits freedom and choice. Debt triggers shame and guilt. Debt causes stress and distrust in relationships. Worry over debt can lead to physical health problems, such as high blood pressure.

Debt makes me irritable, anxious and angry. I'm not alone in suffering from negative emotions related to debt. Research has found links between financial health and mental health.

Researchers from the University of South Hampton who analyzed 65 studies on debt and mental health determined the likelihood of having a mental health problem, particularly depression and anxiety disorders, is three times higher among people who have debt. The link between debt and suicide was especially pronounced: People who committed suicide were eight times more likely to be in debt.

Drug abusers were more than eight times more likely to have debt, and problem drinkers 2.5 times more likely.

Short-term debt, such as credit card debt and overdue bills, was associated with greater depressive symptoms, according to a 2016 study in the *Journal of*

Family and Economic Issues. People in the latter stage of midlife and closing in on retirement, 51- to 64-year-olds, were among the groups where the link between debt and depression was the strongest, along with people who were not stably married and those with no higher than a high school education.

Researchers aren't unified in what causes what – whether stress related to debt causes mental health problems or mental health problems lead to poor financial management. But the two woes are close partners either way.

As midlife progresses, the urgency to escape debt and then keep it at bay increases. Time becomes the enemy; opportunities to get out of debt and recover start to diminish. Wives have been horribly miscast; debt is the real proverbial "ball and chain," and not something one wants to drag into later adulthood.

Whenever I hear that mosquito known as debt whining in my ear, I'm going to slap it silly.

CHAPTER 5

Marriage and Divorce

A Love (Turned Divorce) Story

I never saw it coming. Twice.

Maybe I was oblivious or in denial, or both. But when my ex-wife first announced that she wasn't happy and didn't know if she wanted to stay married, I was dumbfounded. We had two kids under 5 at the time after less than seven years of marriage, and my world was turned upside down in an instant.

I was among the 50 percent of married people who entered marriage thinking divorce was only for other people who marry the wrong person, have poor character or morals, or can't figure out how to make a marriage work, only to end up immersed in the previously unthinkable, bewildered by how such a good thing could have turned so unpleasant.

I didn't want a divorce. When my ex-wife first raised the specter, I struggled to hold on, to determine what the problems were and how to fix them, and to convince my ex-wife to stay in the marriage and work things out. My emotions were raw and unstable. I became depressed. I lost my appetite and energy, had difficulty sleeping, and experienced trouble concentrating at work. I went to a therapist, desperate to have someone objective with whom I could unload and discuss my predicament.

At the same time, I visited a divorce lawyer, because I knew my ex-wife already had. I dreaded the meeting. I dreaded the prospect of being a part-time father and exposing my young children to the perils of divorce.

We went to couples counseling. I vacillated between feeling hopeful and frustrated that my ex-wife seemed entrenched in her position that she was uncertain whether she wanted to remain married and non-committal toward working to save the marriage. We co-existed for several months in an awkward netherworld of fragile uncertainty. I slept in the basement. I tried to find religion, going to Jewish services, partly in search of peace and community and partly just to escape the tension of being home.

And then, gradually, things got better. We seemed to turn a corner toward reconciliation. We made efforts to be more thoughtful of each other and communicate better. We seemed to be committed to making the marriage work. But perhaps something had been broken irretrievably – or perhaps something was broken all along.

Staggered

Less than four years later, after a blowup over a happenstance, comedy-of-errors incident that provoked anger, hurt feelings and resentment, my ex-wife announced she was done. Again, I was staggered. I knew things weren't great, but I also believed they weren't *bad* either, at least *not divorce-worthy*. We weren't blissful, but things seemed relatively smooth, two typically busy parents of an 8- and 6-year-old, juggling parenthood, careers, finances and social lives. Two successive job layoffs I had suffered added stress, but I didn't think they were something the marriage could not handle.

This time, my ex-wife was firm in her resolve. I tried, perhaps foolishly, to hold my ground and influence her to work things out. It didn't work. There was no more trying -- only a long march toward a slow death. During the previous divorce threat, I felt befuddled, depressed and physically sick. This time, I was more prone to outbursts of anger, which I knew were ugly and abhorrent but had trouble controlling. I was so easily set off.

I went through the stages of grief for my marriage – denial, anger, bargaining, depression and finally, acceptance. We lived together for seven months in a state of confrontation, avoidance, resignation and disdain. It was miserable, living with day-to-day tension and knowing what was coming and the eventuality of involving our kids in a breakup. We went to mediation sessions, which I saw as a last ray of hope, but the well was dry. We worked to figure out how to separate amicably.

Finally, we made the arrangement to separate. I stubbornly, and perhaps ill-advisedly, refused to leave the married home. I just didn't want to be the one to leave, to raise the white flag, to say goodbye and give the appearance of walking out on the kids. I also worried that leaving would create disadvantages for me in future legal negotiations.

During our seven-month Cold War, my ex-wife frequently recited the times I had disappointed her, made mistakes or bad decisions or seemed uncaring and unsupportive, adding up to being a less-than-stellar husband. Those incidents couldn't be redeemed; they were etched into the narrative of our marriage. The more I railed against or disputed her accounts, the more despondent I felt and the deeper the hole I dug.

A Love Story...Or So I Thought

Like most marriages, it wasn't all bad – far from it. We had had a delightful love story, or so I believed. We were senior year college sweethearts. We camped out for several days in Provincetown, MA before graduation, and I had never felt happier. We survived a year of long-distance romance, Upstate New York to Florida, before drifting apart because of impracticalities. Six years later, we rekindled the romance after I discovered my ex-wife had ended a long-term relationship and was interested in seeing me. We endured another long-distance relationship, this time more manageable, Maryland to New York, before getting engaged and finally settling in the same place, my ex-wife moving to Maryland. We loved each other – at least, I know I loved her.

As our marriage came crashing down, so did my beliefs about what I thought I understood about our relationship. Was it revisionist history, or the truth from one partner's perspective? My ex-wife said perhaps we should have never married, it was all a mistake, maybe she never really loved me. Perhaps I wasn't the person she thought I was – didn't have the character she was seeking, not good husband material.

At the time we married, I was a *Baltimore Sun* reporter, which sounds prestigious. By the time we separated, I had been severed from *The Sun* during a ruthless round of downsizing, laid off from two other jobs, unemployed, and about to start an uncertain venture as a Baltimore City teacher. Perhaps she grew weary of such instability and lack of focus and contentment. I was searching. Perhaps she gave up too much in leaving her established New York life behind, including a graduate school program, to be with me.

The separation was not without challenges and recurring hurtful feelings, but it was a great relief. However, I felt a sense of failure, shame and embarrassment to be heading toward a divorce. What was wrong with me that I couldn't make my wife happy and keep a marriage strong? The simplest answer, as I have come to realize and accept over the years, is that love – to whatever degree there was that, and I believe there was – just withered, and without it, there just wasn't enough worth salvaging to bind two people together for eternity.

The finiteness of love is the train that I never saw coming through the tunnel. And here's where it seems entirely appropriate to quote Bruce Springsteen's *Tunnel of Love*, his song about an amusement park ride serving as a metaphor for the dark side of a love relationship, my first marriage:

> *...There's a room of shadows that gets so dark brother*
> *It's easy for two people to lose each other in this tunnel of love*
> *Well, it ought to be easy ought to be simple enough, yeah*
> *Man meets woman and they fall in love*
> *But the house is haunted and the ride gets rough*
> *And you've got to learn to live with what you can't rise above*
> *If you want to ride on down, down in through this tunnel of love*

It's So Funny How We Don't Talk Anymore (Ode to Cliff Richard)

Well it really doesn't matter to me.
I guess you're leaving was meant to be.
It's down to you now you want to be free.
Well I hope you know which way to go you're on your own again.
And don't come crying to me when you're the lonely one.
Remember what you've done.
It's so funny how we don't talk anymore.
It's so funny why we don't talk anymore

Cliff Richard, We Don't Talk Anymore

April 2015 -- My ex-wife got remarried two weeks ago. It hardly registered, good, bad or indifferent. Our past time together is so distant now.

We'll be forever connected by our two kids, 19 and 16 (as of 2015). Other than that, I can't say I know her at all anymore. It's strange how someone once so important can become so inconsequential – her to me and me to her – except for the perpetual link. That's just the way it is.

I briefly sensed caring from my ex-wife when my mother died in October 2013 and she attended the memorial. That's the last time. It's strange to feel like you don't matter much to someone when at one time you mattered a lot.

We met at college when we were 19, and dated senior year. She was editor of the college newspaper, the overachiever. I was a writer, not as driven or intense. It was kind of always like that. We went separate ways after college, and after a year, the relationship flamed out.

We rekindled a long-distance relationship at 29, and got married at 30, at our alma mater. It was a pretty cool, lost-and-found love story. It didn't last.

We split up after 11 years in 2005, when the kids were still in elementary school. Eerily, the kids were about exactly the same age as my brother and I when my parents split up. The protracted end was awful. The final break up was a relief.

As the kids have gotten older, we've communicated less and less. I've barely talked to her the last several years. When I do try to discuss something concerning the kids, she usually has somewhere to go, something else to do, another call to make. I'm accustomed to squeezing any conversation into three minutes or less.

Over beers on a trip to Florida with my good friend, when we talk openly about jobs, marriage, kids, sex, and old girlfriends, the topic of my relationship with my ex-wife came up and how well we communicate for the sake of the kids. I told him we've done a really good job. The kids are well-adjusted – one is in college, and the other is on track. Neither has suffered any manifest big problems due to the divorce. We must be communicating well, I told him.

"No, you don't. You don't communicate at all," he assessed. It hit me. He was right. We talk the bare minimum -- the occasional money or scheduling issue.

Maybe that's all there should be between divorced parents. Maybe that's more than a lot of divorced couples. Regardless, it still strikes me as sad that as the parents of two kids, forever joined by that bond, I know so little about how she parents and her thoughts about the kids' futures, their current challenges, how they've changed and adjusted as teenagers, how they can develop their potentials, whether she has any concerns, and if so, how to address them.

I've grown weary of trying to engage. It's easier not to, though it doesn't strike me as the best approach. But maybe this is the way divorce should be. Kind of like none of it ever happened. Everyone moves on. We don't talk anymore.

Overcoming Perils of Divorce

I'm a child of divorce who has wound up raising two children of divorce of my own.

Children of divorce face many more challenges in their development as kids and in adjustments to adult life and adult relationships than children from intact families, as found in Judith Wallerstein's landmark 25-year study, *The Unexpected Legacy of Divorce.*

But so far, at least from what I can observe on the surface and by traditional markers of success, my daughter and son are showing strong signs of overcoming the perils of divorce.

[*Disclaimer: Father's unabashed bragging on kids to follow.*] My daughter, 21, is set to graduate from the University of Maryland in May 2017, with a 3.7 GPA and multiple honor roll appearances. She's run marathons. She's ventured into the world, spending a semester in France and traveling extensively throughout Europe. She has loads of friends, and has formed and maintained an intimate relationship, dating a solid young man for four years. She has an internship with the French Embassy and is planning to teach English in France after graduation.

My son, 18, earned straight As in his first semester at the University of Maryland-Baltimore County (UMBC), taking advanced courses in computer science, biology and math that would have pummeled me as a freshman. He earned multiple Advanced Placement (AP) college credits while in high school, setting him up to graduate college within three years.

He has maintained and thrived in a job while attending college and just celebrated six months in a relationship with a lovely girlfriend.

Psychological, social or emotional problems connected to growing up in a divorced family could surface as they advance into young adulthood, progress deeper into their own relationships and reflect more on their childhood experiences. But to this point, I'm thrilled and grateful for their demonstrated resilience and ability to adapt, thrive and make good decisions.

I will also take some credit for their positive adjustments, and give a good deal to their mother, for making a commitment to positive, caring and mutually respectful and cooperative parenting, despite the challenges we each faced due to the dissolution of our marriage. Both step-parents, Amy and Bernard, also deserve credit for being consistent, stable and positive influences, in roles often fraught with conflict that can become destructive and divisive.

For half or more of their childhoods, the kids split their time – week on and week off – with each parent. There was unavoidable upheaval – my ex-wife and I each moved twice and sold the kids' primary childhood home. But we never lived more than 10 minutes apart (until last year when my ex-wife moved to Texas), and the kids were able to continue attending school in their same district without disruption.

As parents, we cooperated in financial matters, and though we were weaker financially as separate entities, the kids weren't deprived of things they wanted to do and didn't suffer materially. We were each committed to saving for the kids' college educations despite the split, and now that is paying off big-time.

I said things I shouldn't have and made mistakes, especially early in the breakup. Challenges arose throughout our co-parenting in relation to family gatherings, which became emotional and tense. We weathered them, though with impact on the kids.

Overall, however, I strived to be respectful and positive about my ex-wife, and not pollute the kids' minds or attempt to influence them negatively or turn them against their mother with whatever hard feelings I might have had. And for good reason, because I knew my ex-wife was a good mother, and the kids knew the same, and anything I did to tear her down would reflect badly upon me and prompt the kids to resent me. To my knowledge, my ex-wife behaved the same toward me, and I'm grateful for that.

I believe these efforts, which had to be conscious, thoughtful, consistent and enduring, have helped ameliorate the effects of divorce for my two kids. And those potential effects, according to Wallerstein's 25-year study, are considerable and lasting:

- ❖ A harder, unhappier and diminished childhood, including adjustments in contact with each parent, relocations, losses of friendships and activities, decreased influence of parenting, higher anxiety, and worry about one or both parents
- ❖ More acting out and less protection during adolescence, a result largely of inconsistent and unenforced rules and standards, and assuming greater responsibilities for themselves

- ❖ Higher chances of sexual promiscuity among female adolescents
- ❖ A belief that personal relationships are unreliable, and even the closest family relationships can't be expected to last
- ❖ Observations of second parental marriages that typically proved less stable and enduring than the first
- ❖ Feelings of loneliness, bewilderment and anger at parents
- ❖ Scarring memories of witnessing violence during the breakup and aftermath, and repercussions of abandonment
- ❖ Less planning for and lower chances of college enrollment, and inadequate financial support from parents once enrolled
- ❖ Diminished capacity to love and to be loved within a lasting, committed relationship in adulthood, a fear of failure and feelings of pessimism based on their childhood experiences, and a desire to avoid the emotional pain

Though impacts are inevitable, I am hopeful that my kids will avoid or minimize these impacts through their own strengths and abilities to deal with their childhood divorce experience in healthy ways, and through the knowledge that their parents – all four of us now – care about them greatly and always will be there to support them. So far, it looks like that's the track they are traveling, and I am confident that they have the tools and fortitude to stay that course. Hopefully, they will break the familial pattern both my ex-wife and I experienced as kids, and bestowed on our own.

Deep in the Heart of Texas

Even though I've been divorced from my ex-wife for 11 years, we've never lived more than five miles from each other – until now.

Those five miles have become 1,500 miles, as my ex-wife moved to Texas this summer to be with her husband, who was transferred to Houston for his job.

For the first time in those 11 years, my house becomes the sole home base for our two kids, who are both in college in their home state of Maryland.

I always thought I would be the more likely one to move, but things can change fast in life. My ex-wife surprised me and beat me to it. With the kids' mom no longer in the area, I feel some extra sense of responsibility to stay close even as I'm developing a growing sense of wanderlust for a new environment and a fresh start as I transition to a new counseling career after 28 years in Maryland.

My ex-wife's Texas move marks another type of transition. During the kids' years in secondary school, I saw my ex-wife on a regular basis for school events, athletic activities, certain family gatherings and transitions of the kids from one house to another each week. Though we didn't talk a lot, we were cordial and always had the chance to discuss situations concerning the kids when necessary.

Now our estrangement is much more complete, as the saying goes, "Outta sight, outta mind." The combination of both kids' entry into college, my summer away from home teaching tennis at a resort and my ex-wife's move has resulted in minimal communications.

Perhaps that's just the way it is with divorced parents when the kids leave home, but I still believe as parents, we have the common bond of our kids forever and we shouldn't lose touch. We know them best and care about them most. Ideally, I believe we should not be strangers.

But I anticipate being virtually out of touch, now that my ex-wife is Deep in the Heart of Texas.

Midlife Men and Divorce: Risky Business

For the capstone class – the 22nd! – of my 5 ½-year master's degree program in clinical mental health counseling, I had to choose a narrow "clinical population" for a research project. Somewhat shamelessly, self-servingly and unimaginatively, I essentially chose myself: a midlife man who has experienced divorce.

The findings were not pretty for the divorced midlife's male's future, though I acknowledge I intentionally selected research that highlighted why this population would be candidates for mental health treatment.

Research has come to varying and sometimes contrasting conclusions on divorce and midlife men (roughly age 35 to 60), and mitigating factors are difficult to account for.

However, numerous studies have shown that midlife men who have experienced marital breakdown have had greater propensity to become depressed, anxious or develop other psychiatric disorders; abuse alcohol or drugs; suffer from higher rates of illness, earlier death and suicide; harbor anger; live with loneliness and social phobia; qualify for work disability; and experience lower levels of physical health, mental and emotional well-being, and happiness and self-esteem.

And the majority of time, men aren't the ones pulling the trigger on divorce, which studies show is one of the most psychologically distressing events in life. Research indicates that wives frustrated by an inability to improve their troubled marriages may be more likely to end them, with one study concluding that husbands initiate only a quarter to a third of marital separations.

These are research-based outcomes of divorce that pose challenges for the midlife man:

❖ Recently divorced men were more likely than other groups to receive psychiatric treatment and be prescribed medication for mental health disorders. One study concluded that major depression was nine times higher among men who had been separated or divorced compared to stably married and single men.

❖ Remarriage in midlife brings with it a whole new set of complications and negotiations that cause stress, indicating that marriage alone does not prevent mental and physical problems. One study found that remarriage was associated with an increased risk of depression compared with men who remained divorced.

❖ Men often rely on their wives for their social lives and support for their health and emotional well-being, as women generally have stronger social support networks. Without their marriage, men can become prone to social isolation and loneliness.

❖ A common dynamic of divorce is "non-acceptance" of marital dissolution. The ongoing feelings of attachment are associated with depression. The reality for some divorced fathers is continuing angry disagreements with and hostility toward their former wife a decade or more after breakup.

❖ Once divorced, men's physical health can decline, as wives often assume a role for monitoring and influencing their partner's health behaviors.

❖ While women experiencing divorce were at higher risk for mood and anxiety disorders, men were at higher risk for new substance abuse disorders. One study indicated that divorced 46-year-old men comprised a disproportionately higher share of binge and heavy drinkers compared to other groups.

❖ The mortality risk for inconsistently married men (those who had divorced and remarried) was more than 40 percent greater than for consistently married men, and men who were currently separated or divorced had a mortality risk 2.5 times greater than consistently married men.

❖ Men who had been divorced had a higher prevalence of work disability many years after the initial divorce.

As for me, I was the prototype of the midlife divorced male: separated at 42 and divorced at 45 in an action initiated by my ex-wife, with two pre-adolescent kids. I also have remarried, and while my wife Amy has been a wonderful social and emotional support, as the research indicated about wives, the second union has inevitably come with some stress due to new family dynamics and inter-relationships, financial complications and psychological adjustments.

I have avoided many of the pitfalls of the midlife divorced male, such as substance abuse or physical health decline, but did not escape divorce unscathed.

When first threatened with divorce and teetering on the brink, I suffered from depression that affected my appetite, sleep, energy level and concentration. I struggled with non-acceptance when the reality of pending divorce flooded me like an unstoppable tidal wave. I lost a big chunk of my social connections and outlets. Worst of all, it was hard not to feel like a failure at something so important, and as a letdown to my kids.

Researchers have come to different conclusions over whether such a thing as a "midlife crisis" really exists, or whether it is a pop culture phenomenon, especially for men. But there's no doubt that midlife is the time men walk through the landmines of marital upheaval, and when they are most prone to its potentially harmful and long-lasting mental health effects.

Riding the Marry-Go-Round

I'm a two-timer. An encore performer. A twin-biller. A mulligan-taker. A repeat customer. A re-doer. A rider on the marry-go-round. I'm remarried.

I was remarried at 47, placing me among the 16 percent of U.S. men aged 40 to 49 who have been married twice, a figure that climbs to 21.6 percent at 50 to 59 and to 24.6 percent, or nearly 1 out of every 4 men, at 60 to 69, according to the U.S. Census Bureau's 2015 study, "Remarriage in the United States." An even higher percentage of 40-to-49-year-old females, 18.2 percent, have been married twice.

My second wife has watched my two kids, who are now college-aged young adults, grow up since they were 9 and 7, and became their stepmother when they were 14 and 12, heading into the most challenging adolescent years. It requires bravery, patience, tolerance, acceptance, respect, understanding, flexibility, persistence, discipline, forgiveness and the capacity to love to become an effective and enduring stepparent.

Remarriage brings a whole new set of complications and negotiations for the new couple that cause stress:

- ❖ blended families;
- ❖ ex-spouses who may be intrusive;
- ❖ divided loyalties among children and extended family members;
- ❖ ambiguous stepparent roles and expectations;
- ❖ uncertain and evolving children's reactions to changing family dynamics; financial complexities;

- ❖ practical and logistical decisions to reconcile often well-established, separate lives, lifestyles and cultures;
- ❖ trust issues and other emotional baggage; and
- ❖ legal agreements and bleed-over contentiousness from first marriages.

Compared to the virtual blank slate of a first marriage, remarriage can appear an Etch A Sketch on steroids. My second marriage has not been immune from some of these challenges.

If raising kids is the toughest job you could ever have, imagine stepping in as a relief pitcher in the seventh inning, when kids are entering and navigating adolescence as mine were, with all the challenges that raging hormones, establishing independent identities, questioning authority and fitting in with peers presents. A stepparent who adopts an authoritarian approach risks creating an environment of constant tension and turmoil.

On the matter of step-parenting, The Gottman Institute, which researches marriage and relationships, explains the disappointment a stepparent encounters in desiring reciprocal love from stepchildren that may fall short of expectations, and outlines a realistic role: The "role of the stepparent is one of an adult friend, mentor, and supporter rather than a disciplinarian," says the Gottman Institute blog. "There's no such thing as instant love. When stepparents feel unappreciated or disrespected by their stepchildren, they will have difficulty bonding with them – causing stress for the stepfamily."

When a biological parent of the same gender as the stepparent is firmly involved in the family picture and the children's lives, even when not living with them full-time, it may be unrealistic to expect of the children to show equal respect, appreciation and love to each parental figure. A stepparent who keeps score in such ways is setting himself or herself up for disappointment, corrosive resentment and an emotional rollercoaster ride. Children of divorce do their best to cope with confusing and distressing situations and want nothing to do with choosing sides or participating in competitions for their attention and affection, even under the friendliest of circumstances.

Financial issues, which can be vexing in first marriages, can become even more complicated in second marriages. Sharing finances and deciding on financial priorities are aspects of marriage that can produce vulnerability and distrust. These feelings can be amplified in remarriage when one or both partners, often with decades of accumulated assets, debts and obligations, may have children for whom they are financially responsible, child support or alimony payment arrangements, pending college tuition and room and board costs, or property, equity and retirement investments. My second wife married me at a time when I had years of kids' college costs upcoming. In any remarriage, it would be fair to ask: What should be the new stepparent's financial obligation toward the stepchildren's college expenses, if any?

Remarriage is volatile. The odds of second marriages surviving are worse than first marriages. The National

Stepfamily Resource Center cites a divorce rate among individuals who get remarried of 60 percent, while most measures of the divorce rate among first-timers hover around 50 percent. Studies show those who have experienced divorce before are more likely to consider it again when marital struggles emerge. Also, ex-spouse conflicts and new partners parachuting into often ill-defined parenting responsibilities add to the strain that pushes the remarriage divorce rate higher.

Yet those who have lost in love still want to take their mulligans, men more than women. A 2014 Pew Research Center study found that adults who have been previously married are more likely than not to remarry: 57 percent of previously married 35-to-44-year-olds; 63 percent of 45-to-54-year-olds; and 67 percent of 55-to-64-year-olds had remarried. A Pew survey found that only 30 percent of previously married men did not want to remarry, while 54 percent of previously married women indicated they would prefer to remain single, reflecting men's greater needs for the social and emotional support that marriage provides.

Perhaps more than anything, the high rates of remarriage show resiliency of spirit, faith in the institution and the innate desire of humans to connect on a deeper level and share lives, longings that outweigh the challenges of remarriage for many. Apparently, remarriage stands as the poster child for the trite cliché: "If at first you don't succeed, try, try again."

CHAPTER 6

Parenting

5 Basic and Valuable Lessons I've Learned about Parenting

As the younger of my two children closes in on his 18th birthday, I offer five basic parenting principles that I view as important in raising well-adjusted, self-sufficient, industrious and confident children.

I didn't invent them, and by no means was I always exemplary in following these practices -- I had to learn, and still am learning, from my own mistakes and bad habits. Nor are my 20-year-old daughter Rebecca and high school graduate son Daniel perfect or devoid of flaws or insecurities. Neither are your classic All-Americans or stereotypical overachievers. But they are on good tracks in their lives, have done quite well for themselves, and, importantly for me, rarely caused me any worry, grief or stress that more troubled children can cause parents.

I also have realized these aspects of positive parenting in my counseling masters' program and associated internship, where I saw the havoc wreaked by destructive or neglectful parenting.

1. **Express caring, love and pride often.** Parental expression of the positive emotions toward their children can have a lifelong impact on their self-esteem, self-image, confidence, security, well-being and overall feelings about themselves. As long as these expressions of positive emotions are genuine and backed up by actions, I don't think you can overdo it. On the flip side, parents who frequently express destructive emotions and feelings, such as anger and disappointment, or who excessively criticize children through mocking, condescension, belittlement or other abusive behaviors, cause their children great damage that they invariably will carry into adulthood and will have tremendous difficulty in undoing.

2. **Promote independence; let children make their own choices within reason and accept responsibility and consequences.** A relatively new phenomenon in parenting is the "helicopter parent" – those parents who hover over their children and try to protect them from any wrong move or negative consequence and cushion or fix any disappointment, failure or mistake. Kids aren't fragile; they're resilient. But when you hover too much, they don't use their resiliency muscles and they atrophy. As a result, it seems there's a trend toward a large generation of young adults that has trouble breaking away from the

safe cocoon of over-protective or over-indulgent parents. The sooner kids are given responsibility for their decisions, the more they will take ownership over their own lives and the less they will blame others or external forces for whatever doesn't go their way.

3. **Show up...and be present.** There is no better way to let kids know you care about them, and to help them feel attached, secure and loved, than to show up all the time, every day, unless circumstances absolutely prevent it. Show up to elementary school concerts, dance recitals, athletic events, birthdays, sleepovers (not to stay overnight, but when pickup is needed), and all other activities important to your kids. When you show up, provide encouragement and positive feedback, even if you find fault with their "performance" or "effort." You can offer constructive criticism or advice after the positive words, lending your wisdom and experience to aid learning, but not to tear down or damage confidence. And when you do show up, do your best to be truly "present," not distracted or off in your own distant world. Kids will know when you're paying attention.

4. **Model good behavior and caring, respectful relationships.** Kids will model what they observe in the most important relationships in their life – those with their parents. Their behavior, manners,

work ethic, diligence, emotional regulation and respect for others likely will pattern after their parents'. If they see their parents treating each other and other family members poorly or disrespectfully, they likely will display aspects of that behavior themselves within the family and with others.

5. **Live a disciplined life.** As psychiatrist and well-known author Scott Peck wrote in *The Road Less Traveled,* undisciplined parents breed undisciplined children who carry bad habits and behaviors learned in childhood into adulthood. These problems stemming from a lack of discipline that are hard-wired during childhood often are extremely challenging to break and can dog individuals for a lifetime, causing dysfunction that can damage individuals' self-functioning and ruin relationships. Undisciplined parents usually live chaotic lives in unstructured environments that rarely produce disciplined children.

Fatherly Words of Wisdom to a Son

With Father's Day in three days and my son's 17th birthday two days after that, I figured it was as good a time as any to dole out some fatherly wisdom. I gave my son Daniel a heads up that I was thinking of writing about my sage and hard-earned advice, and even offered him a few pearls as a preview to try to get his buy-in. I thought I'd blow him away with profundity, or at least cleverness, but it didn't have that effect – more like, "Yeah, whatever." At least he didn't yawn, or if he did, only mentally.

Whether he wants it or not – and most teenagers don't and I can't blame them and I'm sure I also was that way at 17 -- I'm going to give it to him. Because that's my job, that's what parents do. Here, eat your spinach, it's good for you, and you're going to like it, because I said so, and I know and you don't!

In fairness, he's heard some of this before. And admittedly, not all my insights are deeply profound. And some of these may be more, "Do as I say, not as I do." But I believe when he is an adult, he will hearken back, and realize some of these nuggets actually were on target...and that's why it will be required reading! Eat your spinach! (I actually have semi-required my kids to read certain newspaper articles about young people who have it tougher than them and have had to struggle for everything they get in life.)

The Top 25 Fatherly Words of Wisdom, with some overlap and in no particular order, except the first one, which is meant to be shocking so he'll pay attention to the rest:

1) Nobody gives a crap about you. Yes, this is harsh, overly dramatic, and for those who are even modestly lucky in life, not even true. But we all find out soon enough that the world can be cruel, so we might as well be ready for that.
2) Cultivate your resilience – you'll most likely need it.
3) Be the best friend you can be to your friends and the best relative to your family members.
4) Cherish your significant other/always have their back.
5) Focus on making your life fulfilling, meaningful and enjoyable, not on accumulating (live as Spartan as you can).
6) Develop self-confidence/believe in yourself (and fake it until you make it).
7) Be proactive/avoid passivity.
8) Lead.
9) Be courageous/have courage of your convictions.
10) Find a passion and pursue it.
11) Don't procrastinate.
12) Drink socially, not to get drunk.
13) Eat healthily and exercise.
14) Practice self-reliance.
15) Strive for authenticity.
16) Be bold/take smart risks.
17) Find your own meaning of spirituality.
18) Be generous.

19)   Be compassionate and seek to understand others.

20)   Beware of your anger/deal with it when you know you have it.

21)   Accept responsibility and accountability.

22)   Invest your money early and often.

23)   Invest in yourself and don't shy away from self-promotion (Look out for Number One). No one will do it for you.

24)   Give back to a cause that is close to your heart. You will benefit spiritually and emotionally as much as those to whom you have given.

25)   Embrace the mind-body connection and nurture both – you will need each in good shape for a long time.

Daddy-Daughter Day

What are the odds of a father and daughter graduating from different universities on the same day?

Infinitesimal. But that is what's destined to take place for me and my daughter Rebecca on May 20, 2017, barring unforeseen circumstances.

We're each about to start our final semesters. I'll be graduating from the clinical mental health counseling master's program at Loyola University-Maryland after a 5 ½-year marathon, while Rebecca will be graduating with a bachelor's degree in sociology from the University of Maryland after four years.

It will be a proud day for the Sachs family. Unfortunately, though, I'll have to make a choice, because the graduation ceremonies conflict.

The choice is really no choice at all. As much as I would like to participate in my graduation to savor my accomplishment and sacrifice – and it really has been that, involving a career change, job loss, precipitous drop in income, scrambling to patch together part-time, temporary and seasonal employment, large tuition bills, attending evening classes after work, securing and working at two internships that have tested me, and a long-term commitment to finish rather than quit when feeling overwhelmed – the obvious choice is to attend my daughter's graduation.

It's not that I'm selfless. I'm not. I think a lot about myself. I'm all about me, a lot of the time. I'm not a huge giver. I might not give you the shirt off my back. But May 20 will be my daughter's time. It will be enough for me to know what I accomplished and that I persevered through obstacles, as much as I would like to share that moment with grad school colleagues who have done the same.

It will be more important to me that my daughter knows and remembers that I was there, and to celebrate her achievement. I have tried to do that throughout her 21 years.

There's a quote you might know, often attributed to director Woody Allen, that "90 percent of life is showing up." But apparently what Allen really said was, "80 percent of success is showing up." So if I multiply a .90 show-up rate by a .80 success rate, I have a 72 percent chance of success by showing up at my daughter's graduation. I'll take those odds.

Showing up always been a high priority for me as a parent, and a college graduation is no time to slack off. That simple feat – being present -- was made more challenging over the years since I separated from my daughter's mother when she was only 9, but it was never an excuse.

We had hoped our graduations would be on different days on the same weekend. How cool would it be to attend each other's graduations on successive days? I would like my daughter to see a palpable example that learning, growth, striving and change can happen throughout a lifetime, by observing me graduate. But it wasn't to be.

So I will do what I know in my gut is right and what all good parents should do – no awards or kudos needed – and put my child first.

Facing the Music

As my daughter Rebecca and I were discussing her sociology class on adolescence, she tangentially announced, "You and mom did a good job raising me."

Surprised by an out-of-the-blue compliment, I asked, "What makes you say that?"

My daughter explained that she does not view herself as materialistic, implying instead that she values experiences and relationships above things. We provided for her needs and many wants, but we didn't overindulge, and didn't replace our caring, attention and presence with materials, she was saying.

As a 21-year-old sociology major graduating from the University of Maryland in four days, Rebecca has learned about inequality, justice, race, poverty, privilege, human development and other similar topics, helping her become more insightful and introspective about her own life, and more astute about distinctions among individuals and communities.

I was happy to hear my daughter praise our parenting, since her mom and I broke up when she was 9. My biggest fear about our divorce was that it would cause emotional and psychological problems for my daughter and her younger brother.

"So we did a lot of things right," I said, fishing for more praise.

"Yeah, but not everything," she said, adding the inevitable disclaimer.

"What didn't we do so well?"

"There were things I haven't talked to you about."

We were headed to an Easter celebration, so there wasn't time, and it wasn't the right time, to get below the surface. But I kept the conversation in my memory, committed to return to it.

I did that last weekend, inviting Rebecca to have an open discussion with me as a young adult, reflecting on her experiences as a pre-teen and teenager, the positive and the negative, the gratifying and the disappointing, the supportive and the hurtful.

That conversation, I recognize, will require certain things of me, to be constructive rather than destructive or dismissive: I'll want to approach it as a listener, not a talker, and with an open-minded, non-judgmental, non-defensive attitude. Because I know my temptation, like any parent told in retrospect they weren't as magnificent as they believed, will be to explain or justify or rationalize or correct the record, which would only serve to shut down Rebecca, diminish openness, trust and honesty and invalidate her experiences and feelings. My current training in counseling should help me control such urges.

I would like to give Rebecca the chance to have an open forum with me without fear of reprisal or disengagement. I believe it's important to transition into our adult relationship with everything in the open, past issues revealed and understood, nothing left unsaid, as the foundation for our future interactions and communications. It's the key to an emotionally healthy, genuine father-daughter relationship.

I don't know what she will say to me. I don't know if I'll be surprised. I don't know what emotions it will trigger. But I want to hear it. I know I had good intentions throughout her childhood, and did my best as a father. But I also know I made mistakes. And I know the fact of divorce created situations and triggered emotions that were difficult, or perhaps impossible, to manage without having an impact on the kids.

Facing the music about my role and impact as a divorced (and remarried) father in my daughter's life will increase my awareness and, I hope, strengthen my ability to relate to my daughter. It's worth whatever discomfort or ego deflation it may cause me.

Listening

A follow up to Facing the Music, describing my invitation to have an authentic conversation with my young adult daughter to hear her perspective on growing up in a family of divorce and the mistakes or oversights I may have made during those crucial years of development:

Time was running short, but I didn't want to be a typical "all talk, no do" phony dad. I made my overture for an honest conversation just before I went to the beach for three months to teach tennis. Now I had less than two weeks back home until my daughter Rebecca traveled to France for nearly a year to teach English, and she was busy preparing and doing things with friends and family.

There seems never a good time to have difficult, uncomfortable and potentially distressing conversations. They're easily avoided, and that's what many people do, burying the hurt, anger, disappointment, sadness or other negative emotions until one day they boil over and surface in a torrent, providing release for the emotional-baggage carrier and a knockdown punch for the recipient of the pent-up emotions, unaware of the depth and intensity of feelings. I've been on both the unleashing and receiving ends of the bubbling emotional volcanos, and it's never pretty.

A few days before my daughter jetted off, we found ourselves together at home, and I broached the topic.

Understandably, she was ambivalent about getting into a conversation about past wounds and frustrations before embarking on an adventure of a lifetime. But she started talking, and I listened and asked questions.

I can't reveal the content of what we discussed about our relationship and family life, and the complications and challenges my daughter faced as a child, along with her younger brother, whose parents separated 12 years ago when she was 9 and ultimately divorced. It's too private.

But I can say that at certain times I could have handled things better, that I made some mistakes, and that I was sometimes unaware of – or didn't want to acknowledge – how much the kids observed, heard, knew or perceived, even at relatively young ages. Listening to my daughter's perspective and looking back, I can say how challenging it was for me to balance the needs, feelings, happiness, stability and security of my kids with my own needs, desires and emotions, and to try to lean toward selfless rather than selfish.

Divorce and eventual remarriage created some circumstances that ultimately were going to cause some distress for my daughter individually and in our relationship, no matter what I did or said. The complexities of a marriage breakup and the constantly evolving aftermath can't be fully grasped by a child, whose experience can be like that of a pinball ricocheting within a constrained environment. I experienced the pinball game as a child, and certainly didn't understand everything that was going on with my parents, and now so has my daughter.

The beauty of our conversation was that my daughter was able to tell me some things about what transpired from her perspective, what she experienced and how she felt honestly, and I was able to listen while squelching any tendency to be defensive or critical. We got through it with our relationship intact and expressions of love for each other. I'm hoping our conversation helps set a foundation for our future adult relationship, one in which we can be open and honest with each other without fear that we will be jeopardizing our relationship by revealing our feelings and with knowledge that we love each other unconditionally regardless of any conflicts, hurt feelings or differences that can be addressed and resolved.

So many relationships between fathers and adult children barely break the surface because of the dread of what lies beneath and what digging will unearth, or because of an inability, unwillingness or lack of desire to go deeper. Stoicism and emotional avoidance are drilled into males. I don't want that type of relationship with my kids as they grow into adulthood. I want them to know and understand me, with all my attributes and faults, as I do them. I want us to be able to know and share our emotional selves. The only way to do that is to be emotionally available and vulnerable to them, and to show that I care about and want to know how they feel, and can handle it when they lay it on me.

One takeaway from our conversation is that whatever mistakes I made as my daughter was growing up, I believe that she accepts my apologies, forgives my transgressions, acknowledges that I have tried to be a good and caring father and doesn't expect me to be perfect. Our conversation was a good start toward setting the standard and expectation of our relationship for the future. I'm glad we each took the risk of having it instead of avoiding it.

The Bailout

In my short time as a counselor, I've encountered parents who profess virtual powerlessness in the face of the behavior and choices of their young adult and mature adult children, from their late teens to late 20s.

The child rules the roost, while the parents, frayed, demoralized and depressed, submit to the child's willful and controlling ways. I feel for the parents and their conundrum. It must be a weighty burden to worry ceaselessly about your child, indulge the illusion that one can control their child's fate, bail out the child at every turn, and feel eternally responsible for the child's life choices and outcomes.

At the core of this feeling of parental helplessness is confusion over protecting a child – from danger, failure, mistakes, homelessness or even projected death – versus enabling behavior that avoids individual responsibility and experiencing consequences. Intentions may be good; results are not. Such smothering and shielding behavior on the part of parents contributes to the arresting of the child's growth and development. Twenty-five-year-olds essentially are frozen at 15, having learned how to game one or both parents to their advantage and escape accountability. The longer the pattern continues and the parent remains the bailer, the less motivation the child has to change.

Sometimes, one parent contends, their spouse is to blame for their own helplessness, because the spouse is over-protective and unable to let go. One parent claims to try endlessly to set their stunted child free, but the other parent overrules them, shuts them down and continues down the same corrosive path, as the spurned parent becomes relegated to anemic bystander, tilting at windmills. But this is just an excuse to forgive the method the child uses to manipulate the parents to get what they want, just like the child learned as a little kid. While the parents will blame the child – "He just refuses to get a job, what can you do?!" "I can't believe how she talks to her mother! She has no respect!" – the parents are the ones who fail to unite themselves and stick to any set of boundaries, rules or principles that would render their child's behavior ineffective and counterproductive.

Fear, guilt and a desire to control immobilize the parent from allowing their child to make their own choices, accept responsibility, experience consequences, learn from mistakes and live their own lives. The result is a pattern of co-dependency that is difficult to break. The child never breaks away from at least one parent, while the other parent may become a spare part, suffering in self-imposed silence or virtual exile.

The child depends on the parent to coddle and protect, providing safe haven from having to grow up and contend with an uncertain and uncaring world, from taking a risk, from self-determination. The parent depends on the child's feigned incompetence and irresponsibility to feel needed, helpful and good about himself/herself, to validate their duty as a parent by doing "anything" for their child, to fulfill the role of protector and savior.

Adults in their 20s who are capable of living independently are essentially rewarded for their "failure to launch." They don't need a job because their basic financial needs – shelter, food, electricity, water, health care – are provided, as are wants such as cable TV and a car. So they don't bother to seek one; holding a job would require taking individual responsibility. They don't attend school because they have no motivation to set goals. They live at their parents' home because it's a safer bet – all the accountability is heaped on the parents -- and easier. The unavoidable hassles and conflicts with the parents and turmoil in the household are just part of the bargain. They bum money as needed, claiming it is for one purpose while in some cases the parents providing the money know all along it is for drugs or alcohol, and resent giving in, but give in they ultimately do to maintain the dependent relationship.

A young adult living with their parents is a prevalent U.S. social trend: The U.S. Census Bureau found that more than one-third of people aged 18 to 34 lived under their parents' roof in 2015; 10 years earlier, the percentage was about one-fourth. Nearly 9 of 10 who had lived with their parents in 2014 still did a year later. Indicating a rise in parental bailouts, the survey ominously found that 1 in 4 young adults aged 25 to 34 living in their parents' home neither attended school nor worked.

I am grateful and proud that my kids are heading toward independent lives, on schedule. My 22-year-old daughter graduated college and is teaching in France.

My 19-year-old son is attending college, majoring in computer science, and working part-time for UPS in logistics. If one of them holed up in my basement and refused to crawl out into their own life, I can't be sure what I would do. I would hope I wouldn't cave in and cater to dysfunction, irresponsibility and manipulation, but until you walk in someone else's shoes…Thankfully, I don't think my kids will give me the chance to wear those shoes.

One school of therapy posits that all human motivation is intentional, that all behavior is purposeful. Human behavior seeks to shape the world to satisfy at least one human need. For adults who have failed to launch, that need often is self-preservation. The anxiety and doubt of relying on oneself breeds dependence and escape from responsibility. Their behavior sends the message that the world is a scary place that expects something from us; the goal is to remain safe and preserve ego. If you don't attempt, you can't fail. Parents who are too willing to satisfy the need become the enablers who perpetuate their adult children's prolonged adolescence.

CHAPTER 7

Kids: Growing Up, Moving On

The Marathoner: Coming a Long Way

I'm going to try to tear my 19-year-old daughter Rebecca away from college and sorority life for a night to see McFarland USA, the movie about a white coach at a predominantly Latino California high school who struggles to connect with students until he discovers a group of great runners, and builds a championship cross-country team with a long-enduring legacy from nothing. I figure it will have some shared meaning for us, with the importance that cross country has played in Rebecca's life and my small role – at least I like to believe – in making it happen.

Rebecca was never a star athlete. She stuck with soccer longer than I thought she would, long enough to make an "A" team in eighth grade. But she never gelled with her new teammates, and after one fall season, she was done. In a soccer-mad county with intense competition, high school soccer was realistic only for the most talented and dedicated.

That summer before ninth grade I talked to Rebecca about considering running cross country in high school. I had done a couple of slow 5K road races with her before. Her mother is a big-time runner – not fast, but extremely disciplined and relentless – who has a number of marathons to her credit, so Rebecca always had that role model.

I played tennis through high school. After I saw my younger brother join the cross country team and enjoy the camaraderie and inspiration from the group effort and make long-lasting friends, I wished I had done the same. Remembering my brother's rewarding experience, I thought Rebecca could benefit the same way.

But my periodic reminders that summer before ninth grade to Rebecca about the valuable experiences of cross country and if she was considering it at all, the need to train at least a minimal amount, seemed to be more annoying to her than helpful. Maybe that's the inevitable reaction of a 13-year-old daughter to the advice of a father who claims wisdom from experience. Rebecca would respond anxiously that I was stressing her out with all that talk about going out for cross country and training, so I tempered my fatherly advice with backing off.

When mid-August came, I had no idea whether Rebecca would go to cross country tryouts. She did. I feared she wouldn't survive a week in the humid, 90-degree heat with what little training she had put in. She did. There was a time-trial within the first week. I believe Rebecca missed the designated cutoff time, but not by much. But the great thing about cross country is there were no cuts. Perseverance, commitment and determination were rewarded, and whoever stuck with it long enough inevitably improved, and in almost all cases, greatly. That's what Rebecca did.

I remember doing a few organized runs with Rebecca early in her high school cross country career, including one on a high school cross country course, where she would break down with a debilitating pain part way through, usually a cramp in the side, or have trouble breathing. I tried to be caring, but I was also frustrated when it happened. She should have kicked me in the ass for that. Sometimes the pains would happen at meets I attended.

But as her career went on and her body developed and got stronger and adapted to the rigors of the sport, those incidents faded. She became a top-10 runner on her team, a leader in spirit activities, and ultimately a captain. She improved her times for the 5K (3.1-mile) course by about 8 to 10 minutes from freshman to senior year.

Perhaps most importantly, she made great friends on the team who constituted her social circle for four years – all of them excellent students and the type of kids a parent would want their own kid to hang out with. Also importantly, I believe cross country played a major role in increasing Rebecca's self-esteem, self-confidence, intrinsic motivation and work ethic.

This is what I couldn't have predicted more than five years ago when I felt I was on the verge of badgering my daughter to do something she didn't want to do: She not only persisted at cross country, but she has become an accomplished distance runner in an amazingly short time, while carrying a full load as a full-time college student.

She has quickly built up over the past two years by running 10-mile events, half-marathons (13.1 miles), and metric marathons (16-plus miles). Then, in 2014, she announced she was going to run the Baltimore Marathon in October. I thought it might be a little too much to undertake as a college student, but she persisted, training with a group of adult marathoners all summer.

She finished the marathon in just over four hours, a month shy of her 19th birthday. How many 18-year-olds have a marathon to their name? I was proud to see her coming into the homestretch, heading toward the finish at the Baltimore football and baseball stadium complex, looking strong. She wasn't trudging, either. I ran down the sidewalk for a ways to parallel her, and the pace was fast.

So hopefully we will share McFarland USA together, and reminisce about where Rebecca started and her running journey since then. It seems selfish to want to take a small bit of credit, but that's my ego talking. Sometimes I like to know I did something right as a father, and whether Rebecca really needed a little push from me or not, I'd like to think I had a positive influence that has helped her enjoy and benefit from one of the most positive influences in her young life.

Fly Free Kids, Fly Free!

January 1, 2016 -- It's a new year, and things are new, especially for my kids.

The little ones are growing up and fleeing from the nest, and there's nothing I can do about it!

In 12 days, my 20-year-old daughter Rebecca, a student at the University of Maryland, will board a plane for France and a semester abroad. I'm proud of her for being curious and adventurous, and I'm glad to support her experience attending college in France and traveling throughout Europe. I'm sure it will be an experience that will last her a lifetime, which has more value than any other way you can spend money beyond your basic survival needs.

But I'd be lying if I said I wasn't just a little worried about the terrorist activity in that part of the world, with the attacks on Paris nightspots and the Charlie Hebdo newspaper. Thanks ISIS devotees, I'm sure your benevolent God would be pleased to know us parents sending kids to Europe for an education and to see the world have a little more reason to worry, other than just being an ocean away. Mission accomplished!

Regardless, I predict my daughter will return speaking fluent French, with international contacts for her Facebook account, cravings for tartar and newfound confidence for navigating the world.

My 17-year-old son Daniel, who also just gained admission to the university of his choice for Fall 2016 (and even got some scholarship money to boot!), got his driver's license just over a month ago. Since then, he's been a social maven, driving himself to all manner of social gatherings, and even going clothes shopping for himself at the mall. He's been given the responsibility and trust to be independent.

My kids, who I remember driving me crazy as I tried to corral them in the grocery store as 4- and 2-year-olds, running down aisles and toppling piles of boxes on shelves, are most assuredly growing up and on their way to becoming self-sufficient, productive young adults. I'm proud of them for that, and will shamelessly take a little credit for myself for providing at least adequate parenting.

I don't believe in being a "helicopter parent," hovering over the offspring to try to solve all of their problems and protect them from any mistakes. I believe in giving them their independence and responsibility, allowing them to make their own choices (within reason, while they are still attached to their parents financially), and keeping unnecessary worrying to a minimum.

That means one thing, unless or until there is a major hiccup that absolutely requires a helicopter rescue: **Fly free kids, fly free!**

The Empty Nest

Recently, when I've told people what my kids are doing – and even what I'm doing for the summer -- some have made a comment like, "Oh, so you're going to be an empty-nester."

I've never thought of it that way. That's what you call old people in 55+ Senior Living Communities who play a lot of golf and tend to their gardens. At least, that's the image "empty nest" conjures.

But I'm in the midst of a milestone week of activities that serve as markers letting me know that the "empty nest" status, while not fully realized, is progressing toward inevitability unless we suffer a "failure to launch."

The thought of it makes me wistful for my own relative youth as a newer parent and for the times when my kids (seemingly) needed me more. Maybe they'll still need me — or better yet, want me — as an integral part of their lives through their process of leaving the nest. I'm confident we've done our best as parents and the kids are ready to move on as they should with their lives as we adapt to new roles and arrangements.

My son Daniel attended his senior prom on May 20, 2016 and will be graduating high school on May 25, 2016. He looked great, a handsome young man in his tuxedo with the purple vest, bow tie and kerchief to match his date's dress.

I'm proud of Daniel. He assumed a heavy academic load in high school, taking many Advanced Placement and Honors classes, and earning college credits through AP exams and several community college courses. He certainly took on more academic challenges than I ever did, which is perhaps also a sign of the increased pressures placed on kids today and more intense competition, and handled them with confidence and a cool resolve. He was admitted to the university of his choice, and received some scholarship money, for which I am both proud and grateful.

He also became more engaged socially. I could see his growth and development, and more of his personality emerging as he matured from a freshman to a senior. He joined about 30 classmates for a pre-prom party (and parents' photo-shoot marathon). It was a joy to see him interacting with so many friends and acquaintances.

He also recently got his first job at a restaurant, taking on adult responsibilities and earning his keep, another sign of the bird discovering its wings to escape the nest.

And of course, there's Senior Week at Ocean City, MD in early June, the rite of passage. There will be debauchery, but I'm not worried about Daniel. He has a good head, thinks independently and makes his own decisions. I just told him to "be smart." His step-grandma was sterner and put it another way: "Don't be stupid!"

My daughter Rebecca has been spreading her wings for a while, most recently all over Europe while on a college junior year study semester abroad in Lyon, France. She'll return at the end of May, and surely will be busy reconnecting with friends, looking for work and arranging senior year.

I'll be teaching tennis this summer 2016 in Bethany Beach, DE, as part of my career transition to counseling, while on break from classes and internships. The kids will be bouncing this summer from their mom and step-mom, and traveling with friends. I'll come home to visit, and hopefully they can visit me at the beach.

So we'll be scattered and all pursuing our own more independent lives this summer. I'm anticipating the idea of an "empty nest" may start sinking in.

Going, Going, Gone!

Fall Semester 2016 -- A week ago I lugged my son Daniel's mini-refrigerator and cartful of computer equipment to a cramped dorm room at the University of Maryland-Baltimore County (UMBC) and officially became an empty nester. My daughter Rebecca left home for good later the same weekend to move into her new apartment at the University of Maryland.

Since I've been gone all summer scraping together income to fuel my midlife career transition odyssey – except for one-day-per-month visits back home – teaching tennis at the Sea Colony Tennis resort in Bethany Beach, DE, the kids' flight hasn't fully registered with me yet. But when I return home for good on Labor Day night, I'll be faced with the fact that my role as a parent has changed.

My kids have become so much more independent in the last year. Rebecca spent a semester in France and traveled throughout Europe. Daniel became more social, broadened his circle of friends, with whom he traveled to Ocean City, MD for Senior Week and California over the summer, connected with a steady girlfriend, got his first job at which he is advancing and earned college scholarship funds.

They're becoming young adults, and our relationships will change. I am curious what those relationships will be like.

Since they are attending colleges nearby, they'll be around on occasion, but now their college residences are their primary addresses. I am going to miss having one or both kids around the house on a regular basis.

I'm thinking the transition may be easier for me than for parents in an intact family. My kids lived with me only half the time for about half of their childhoods, since they were 9 and 7, because of my divorce. I always felt sad when I brought the kids back to their mom's on Sunday evenings after a week with me, knowing I was going back to an emptier house and that I would likely only see them one time over the next week for dinner. The necessity to adjust to the back and forth, every other week arrangement I hope will help me adapt to this new transitional scenario.

Still, there's nothing like your kids branching out on their own and establishing their independent lives to let you know you are advancing to new and later stages of life.

I taught many kids tennis this summer and met their parents. I couldn't help thinking those parents were me a decade ago, enjoying family vacations at the beach and doing fun kid things like walking the boardwalk at night and sliding the water park during the day. When I told tennis parent clients that I had kids also, though older at 20 and 18 and in college, I had a hard time believing it myself.

Rebecca has talked about becoming a teacher recently and of possibly following her boyfriend, a chemical engineering major, to some yet to be determined destination after college. Daniel will be pursuing studies in the computer science field at a university known for its strength in that area. They both have promising futures. I'm proud of how they have developed and the people they are. I hope I have had a positive influence on them and will remember some of dad's "pearls of wisdom" that they probably didn't want to hear when I offered. I implored both kids to take Spanish; they each took French. I think Daniel already may be happy that I highly recommended dorm life to him when he was considering other college living arrangements.

I look forward to developing and nurturing close and warm adult relationships with both kids. I hope it happens. It will be a two-way street from here on out. Both kids will have to desire that too and give our relationship love and care to help it grow as we all mature.

The kids are gone and one long and crucial part of my parenting journey is over. It's been a challenge, a great learning experience, an honor and a joy, but also tinged with some tumult, sorrow and readjustment resulting from the family breakup and my second marriage. I am eager to see what the next phase will bring and know I will need to work at staying connected.

The kids are gone. In the coming weeks, I'll learn how prepared I am to accept it.

Learning the Value of Work, Intrinsic Motivation

I put on a jacket I hadn't worn in nine months, stuck my hand in the pocket and pulled out a forgotten, folded paper. It was a job application form that hadn't been filled out for Grotto Pizza, a popular chain in Delaware beach towns that recently expanded into our Maryland suburb. My find triggered the memory of a conversation my wife Amy and I had with our son Daniel in the car on our way to dinner at the pizza chain where I had picked up the application.

The gist of the conversation that March 2016 evening was that we expected Daniel to work after he graduated high school later that spring. I advised that the new pizza restaurant was looking for employees and recommended he fill out an application. Daniel expressed resistance to working – or perhaps just to me suggesting where he should work or what he should do – advocating for a last summer before college of doing whatever he wanted.

It got a little tense before we got to the restaurant, Amy and I frustrated at Daniel's nonchalant attitude toward working and earning money for himself. We were concerned about him adopting an attitude of privilege.

For a couple of years, I had recommended to Daniel that he get certified as a lifeguard because we live in a community with 23 pools, or that he work at a summer camp. But he didn't take up my suggestions. Lifeguarding would be boring, and he didn't want to deal with younger kids, he said.

So imagine my surprise when a month after our frustrating conversation, Daniel announced that he had found a job opening on his own and had an interview scheduled at Shophouse, the Asian equivalent of Chipotle Mexican Grill, also owned by Chipotle. He had two interviews, including a group interview with the whole staff to evaluate whether he would fit in, and got the job.

A second surprise came at the end of summer 2016. Daniel easily could have decided it was nice having his first work experience, but he was done with that chapter and on his way to college. Instead, he decided he would keep his job while going to school.

He has been like a utility infielder at Shophouse, working the grill, preparing food, explaining the menu and serving food on the line to customers, and operating as cashier. He is working his way to a promotion to kitchen manager.

I dropped in one night for dinner, where he made me a chicken with peanut sauce bowl. I watched him serve customers, thinking he had come a long way in working with adults and learning about the responsibilities of a job.

He is developing a good work ethic, always arriving to work on time, doing whatever he is asked to do and embracing the team concept of his employer. He also is learning about saving and the value of money, spending on things that are important to him but saving most of what he earns for the future. He earned straight A's during his first semester of college while holding down his job.

I am proud of the way Daniel has embraced his job and the pride he shows in his work and earning his own way, while juggling a rigorous academic load. I am cheered that he is learning about the concepts of individual responsibility, quality of work, working as part of a team and his ability to direct his life with his choices, work ethic and attitude. He already has started applying for summer internship jobs in computer science, his chosen field. His self-motivation has blossomed.

Several times with my kids, they have gone on to do things I had wanted and encouraged them to do, but they did it on their own and in their own way and time, not in direct response to or because of my nudging or urging, or so it has seemed, though maybe my fatherly advice and wisdom had an influence. I've always told my kids that it is preferable when they do things out of intrinsic motivation – based on their own desires and interests – rather than out of extrinsic motivation, such as pleasing their parents and getting the old fogies off their backs. I'm glad they are learning this lifelong lesson, as Daniel's employment endeavor indicates.

(Not) A Chip off the Old Block

Academically, my son Daniel doesn't take after me – except for the fact that we have each attended college. And in today's increasingly specialized and technological economy and job market, I'd say that's good for him.

As a freshman computer science major and bioinformatics minor, Daniel is taking a heavy dose of computer programming, biology, statistics and math. I predict he will separate himself from the masses who hold college degrees, which no longer guarantee entry into the professional world, by going the STEM (Science, Technology, Engineering, Math) route and will find himself in demand in the job market. No post-college Parental Unit Domicile (PUD) basement-dwelling likely or necessary for him!

I, on the other hand, took an occasional math or science course three decades ago at my liberal arts college – only enough to meet the requirements to graduate – and overdosed on philosophy, history, political science, economics and English courses, emerging with a smorgasbord-style International Relations degree that led to nothing in particular. But in that era, being a generalist with a broad liberal arts education could still work as a professional launching pad for many occupations.

It's not that it can't work today, but it just appears harder. Industries can be more selective in hiring graduates who more closely fit the profile for their jobs based on their degrees, internship experiences and technical and industry-specific knowledge. Those without more targeted, specialized and immediately marketable degrees will flood the "generalist" markets, like education, communications, sales, fundraising and social services, creating the immense competition that has left many college graduates on the sidelines.

While teaching tennis at a beach resort last summer in the midst of my career transition to counseling, I talked with a doctor at Minnesota's renowned Mayo Clinic after a tennis clinic. His wife also was a physician. He had two kids in college, and explained his parenting philosophy about his kids' college education.

He did not take a *laissez faire* approach, like many parents who allow their kids to "find themselves" – or not – by experimenting and dabbling with a variety of subjects with no clear idea of where they were heading. Guessing and floundering, and possibly wasting time and money, was not acceptable, he emphasized. If his kids were going to attend college, he demanded that they have "skin in the game" and demonstrate a well-thought out plan outlining what they would study, and how their field of study would lead to a career path and jobs immediately after college, based on real-world economic and occupational data. Otherwise, the parental money pipeline would be disconnected.

It made sense to me. And immediately after my discussion with the doctor, I was struck by pangs of guilt: My daughter Rebecca was about to enter her senior year of college as a liberal arts major – sociology and French minor – and I had never really had that practical conversation with her about the real-world application of her college pursuits. I was the *laissez faire* parent!

That's not necessarily a bad approach. There's value in allowing your kids to make their own decisions, find their interests and passions on their own, and take responsibility for the outcomes. Parents who foist their own interests, desires and fears upon their kids to either force or influence them to take a certain path rarely works – at least not over the long haul – and typically ends in resentment. But I still felt remiss about possibly leaving Rebecca unprepared for a world that can be callous and crush souls.

So I called Rebecca that August day, knowing that merely mentioning the idea of developing a plan for her post-college life early in her senior year could ratchet up her stress level. She assured me that she was considering various ideas and researching careers, and that she wasn't approaching her pending graduation flippantly.

That was enough for me. I could check off the Parental Duty box next to "Advise Child of Importance of College Choices." I've never been a hard-ass parent. I have confidence Rebecca will find her way, just like I do with Daniel.

And even though their career paths will be different, I'm glad both will be making their decisions based on what they want to do, not based on my ideas of what they should do or on pursuing a path based on fear that they won't succeed. Because they will succeed if they have the desire and interest.

There are no strings attached to my investment in their college educations. I'll guide where I can and when and if I'm asked. Otherwise, they're on their own, and I know that's the way they want it.

She's Leaving on a Jet Plane: No Failure to Launch

My daughter literally has launched herself into adulthood.

The cornerstone job as a parent is to help your kids launch themselves successfully into adulthood by fostering their independence, confidence, self-identity, decision-making ability, sense of responsibility and motivation – traits which they have to develop themselves but over which parents have a big influence.

I'm proud and excited to see my 21-year-old daughter Rebecca exhibiting these traits. She has jetted off for Toulon, France, on the Mediterranean coast, for an eight-month assignment teaching English in two French middle schools, her first professional job after graduating college. This will be her second tour abroad, following a semester in college in which she studied at the University of Lyon in Lyon, France, and traveled throughout Europe.

Rebecca landed in Toulon September 18, 2017, not knowing anyone, same as when she ventured to Lyon in a study group comprised of American students from across the country. She was anxious and excited, the eagerness and thrill of the adventure, opportunity, unknown and challenge far outweighing any fears and doubts. I congratulate Rebecca on her adventurous spirit and desire to explore the world.

No *Failure to Launch* here, unlike Matthew McConaughey's 30-something character in the 2006 movie of that title, who resisted leaving the comforts of the cushy life provided by his parents until they hatched a plan to finally get him to launch out on his own.

Psychology Today labeled "failure to launch" as a syndrome characterized by the "difficulties some young adults face when transitioning into the next phase of development—a stage which involves greater independence and responsibility." Energy, desire and motivation are the necessary ingredients to fuel the launch and overcome fears and anxiety, and taking risks and actions comprise the launch process. Then, resilience and perseverance are required to overcome inevitable turbulence during this stage. Without those components, the post-adolescent risks becoming stuck and dependent.

Ultimately, says *Psychology Today* author and psychiatrist Robert Fischer, M.D., for a successful launch, a young adult "must tap into and identify a passion or passions, experience the joy that comes with expressing those passions, and have opportunities to share this joy with others. There must be a conscious effort to cultivate not just the logic of the mind, but also the desires of the heart."

I'm gratified that Rebecca is following her passion and desire by taking the risk and action to travel to France and to teach in foreign schools.

Rebecca is part of an age group that has been segmented recently from the broader adulthood category and coined "emerging adulthood" for its characteristics common to people in their late teens through their 20s. These are young people who feel like the knot in a tug-of-war rope, caught between breaking free of the challenges of adolescence yet often still maintaining close bonds with parents, family and the familiar trappings of youthful existence.

The psychologist who identified the new life-span development phase, Jeffrey Arnett, outlined five distinct features of emerging adulthood:

- ❖ **Identity exploration:** Establishing one's self-identity continues to evolve throughout the 20s, as young adults search for what brings satisfaction out of education, work, and relationships.

- ❖ **Instability:** This group moves around a lot, among schools, jobs, locations and residences as they experiment with future paths, change their minds and directions and struggle to accumulate the resources to fuel their journeys.

- ❖ **Self-focus:** Emerging adulthood is a time of intensive internal focus, as young adults explore their desires for work, living arrangements, experiences and relationships with a sense of broad possibilities and few encumbrances. It is an age when opportunities may seem limitless, before developments such as marriage, children, increased financial obligations and career choices inevitably pose constraints and redirect attention more outward.

- ❖ **Feeling in between:** Emerging adults feel they are taking more responsibility for their own lives and decisions, yet still feel they have not completely broken free from some form of dependence and do not completely feel like an entirely self-sufficient, autonomous adult.

- ❖ **Age of possibilities:** Optimism characterizes emerging adulthood. After taking a hard look at their parents' lives, many believe they have a good chance to create a more rewarding and exciting life for themselves.

Another researcher sought to determine why some emerging adults thrive and why some struggle in establishing identities and independence. She found that the foundation for such progress or obstacles are established in childhood and adolescence, and are heavily influenced by parents striking the right balance between providing support and structure, and encouraging kids to pursue independence and make their own decisions.

One type of family dysfunction that inhibits emerging adults from becoming independent is "enmeshment," when family members' emotional lives are so intertwined that children have difficulty separating, becoming their own person, and accepting responsibility for their choices and lives. This is a dynamic I have observed often in counseling.

The signs are clear that my daughter is becoming the captain of her own jet. I feel rewarded as a father that I have contributed to the foundation of her launching pad.

What Brown Can Do for Me

What can Brown do for me?

Brown can hire my son and give him real-world, corporate, big-business experience in his chosen field in college; offer him a sturdy rung on the base of the career ladder; teach him about the discipline, responsibility, accountability, integrity, honesty, teamwork and communications that comprise effective work environments; play a role in his maturation; and help him build a financial nest egg before launch into the adult world, all while he is still a teenager. That's what Brown can do for me – and my 19-year-old son Daniel.

After years of watching United Parcel Service's (UPS) television ads asking, "What can Brown do for you?" and seeing the brown vans with the brown-clad delivery personnel rolling through my neighborhood, I never expected that the world's largest package delivery company and provider of supply chain management solutions would be hiring my son as a college freshman to assist with its information technology and data management operations.

For some time as a high school senior, Daniel seemed indifferent about work. But he made a 180-degree turn in his attitude, initiative and motivation, without undue parental pressure or requirements.

He started during his senior year in high school as a restaurant worker, preparing food and grilling in the kitchen and helping customers behind the service counter. To my surprise, he chose to maintain his job after enrolling as a freshman at the University of

Maryland-Baltimore County (UMBC), even though his employer was 30 minutes away from campus. He kept that job for nearly his entire freshman year.

In his freshman spring semester, Daniel, a computer science major, attended a job fair on campus, connecting with UPS, which hired him as an intern. Among the benefits of an internship at UPS are that the position is paid, and it lasts more than a semester, or even a year. UPS's internship can last throughout a college career, as the company uses its internship program as a recruitment tool for grooming future full-time employees.

Of course, since Daniel is a computer science major taking a full load of computer systems, math, informatics and science courses, and I am a liberal arts major who has worked in journalism, public relations and the social sciences, I have a hard time understanding what he is doing day-to-day. But this is what I got from his description: Daniel works in the world of Big Data, which Wikipedia describes as "data sets that are so large and complex that traditional data processing application software is inadequate," and includes challenges such as capturing data, data storage, data analysis, search, sharing, and other functions. As someone who is perplexed by Small Data, I am quite impressed.

As Daniel describes it, he is an application developer who deals in the areas of customer engagement and quality control. He tracks and monitors UPS data centers and deals with code that helps keep track of data. He helps ensure that UPS's delivery technology is working for its customers. He is a trouble-shooter.

As a father, I am proud and gratified to see my son holding down a professional job, working as a colleague with adults, becoming more independent, developing a work ethic, learning the value of earning a living and of saving for the future, investing in himself, juggling work and school, and evaluating through experience what he would like to do with his career before he is tossed into "the real world."

Many young adults wind up directionless in their 20s, and squander precious time trying, sometimes unsuccessfully, to identify interests and passions, and how those can translate to making a living, or in working in dead-end jobs in which they have little interest or future. I know a few fathers whose sons have dealt with these challenges, and both the fathers and sons have had difficult times as a result, both as individuals and in their relationships.

So what can Brown do for me? Quite simply, it is helping my son get a good start on his adult life, which brings me peace of mind. And that's invaluable for a parent.

CHAPTER 8

Mental Health and Counseling: Mental, Emotional and Spiritual Well-Being

The Rewarding Work of Helping People Change Their Lives

Until you work in a mental health setting, you never realize the prevalence of depression, anxiety, mood and attention deficit/hyperactivity disorders, trauma, substance abuse, paranoia, anger issues, family dysfunction and other mental health problems in our society.

In the midst of a career transition from public relations to counseling, I just completed the first year of my internship at an outpatient mental health clinic that served Medicaid recipients for my counseling degree program. I counseled people with all those issues. All took medications as part of their treatment. Therapy was the other half of their recovery and managing their symptoms.

Gaining better awareness of ourselves and understanding our current behaviors and how the past may have affected them can be a lifelong and complex process.

At the risk of oversimplification, recovery and a more healthy and satisfying life for people suffering from mental health issues (excluding those without severe mental illness or psychosis) comes down to several key factors:

- ❖ Desire and readiness to change
- ❖ Commitment to take actions
- ❖ Ability to implement new ideas or behaviors
- ❖ Willingness to accept reality
- ❖ Fortitude to replace negative or destructive thoughts with more positive ones

I found clients were able to change their thinking and behaviors, and as a result, their feelings and emotions, to varying degrees and on different timetables. One client reported she had consciously changed a negative pattern of thinking to a more positive one within a few weeks, and as a result had significantly reduced stress and anxiety and slept better. Her entire presentation changed from forlorn and dragging to bright and eager. That told me clients had the ability to make rapid and meaningful changes. When you observe someone change like that, it's a beautiful thing.

Others struggled with the same issues of anxiety, anger or dependency for months with small improvements and back slides. They had walls that were harder to penetrate, built over lifetimes of learned behaviors, ingrained messages and adaptations to survive circumstances.

Overall, the internship provided a fascinating window into the human experience and human behavior through my adult and child clients and their families. It was a privilege to get to know them, and difficult to tell them I had to leave when my internship ended.

The internship also taught me how little I know about mental health disorders and strategies to help people who suffer from them. There's so much to learn about the science and art of mental health and therapy. And about how to be comfortable just being with people, showing authentic caring, developing a connection and earning their trust. But I'm learning, and excited about expanding my knowledge, getting better at being helpful and more courageous about challenging people to dive deeper below the surface to confront the roots of their problems. All signs indicate it will be a rewarding new career. I'm glad I took that gamble.

Choose It or Lose It

...[E]verything can be taken from a man but one thing: the last of the human freedoms—to choose one's attitude in any given set of circumstances, to choose one's own way. And there were always choices to make. Every day, every hour, offered the opportunity to make a decision...

Viktor Frankl, Man's Search for Meaning

...[F]or all practical purposes, we choose everything we do, including the misery we feel. Other people can neither make us miserable nor make us happy...[W]e choose all our actions and thoughts and, indirectly, almost all our feelings and much of our physiology. As bad as you may feel, much of what goes on in your body when you are in pain or sick is the indirect result of the actions and thoughts you choose or have chosen every day of your life...[W]e are much more in control of our lives than we realize. Unfortunately, much of that control is not effective...Taking more effective control means making better choices...

William Glasser, MD, A New Psychology of Personal Freedom

In the 1990s, I attended the Landmark Forum, a three-day workshop designed to bring about transformative changes in the quality of one's life through an examination of, and shifts in one's beliefs, thoughts, behaviors, patterns, commitments and actions.

A Forum anecdote that I remember 20 years later is "Flat tire. Choose." The premise is simple: Your car gets a flat tire on an inconvenient stretch of road. The choices are more complicated: bash the steering wheel; kick the tire; bang the hood; Frisbee the hubcap; yell and scream; drop some F-bombs; curse the gods and your perpetual bad luck; cry; sit on the side of the road in misery or bewilderment. Or, choose to accept reality and make decisions to address the problem. It's your choice: Choose...

I have no choice. How many times have you heard that grievance? Is it *ever* really true?

We all have choices, all the time. Even when it seems like we don't have any. Even when it seems we have no *good choices*, when choices are constrained, we still have choices, the free will to choose. We can choose our attitude, our perspective, our response, our outlook, our meaning. We can choose not to choose, and still make a choice.

We can even choose our feelings, contends the founder of reality therapy and choice theory, William Glasser, MD, who would say that an individual is "depressing," or "saddening," indicating that they are consciously choosing their mood state and have the power to make a different choice.

According to Glasser's choice theory, all human behavior is intentional, not aimless, and choices are based on "here-and-now" motivations.

Choices are made to generate feedback from the outer world and satisfy what Glasser defined as the five basic human needs: survival, love/belonging, power, freedom/independence and fun. Choices also are made to send a message to the outer world, and to specific individuals with whom one has a relationship; for example, that one is confident or self-doubting, happy or angry, trusting or distrustful, constructive or self-destructive, hungry for success or resigned to failure.

Psychiatrist Viktor Frankl, a World War II Holocaust survivor who spent years in a Nazi concentration camp, described the realization that he had choices – his belief in his own self-dignity, and what he could think, envision and hope, for example -- despite the brutal and horrific conditions he endured as a captive as a main reason for his survival. Recognizing the freedom to choose was a prime factor that separated those who maintained a sense of meaning in their lives and hope for the future, and those who became deadened to life, devoid of faith and more likely to succumb to death, Frankl wrote in *Man's Search for Meaning.*

I have observed as a mental health counselor that the execution of choice in people's lives – the willingness to use it proactively and the effectiveness with which it is used – is perhaps the greatest determiner of an individual's mental and emotional health, the condition of their relationships and their ability to create meaning and purpose in their lives.

Husbands and wives decline to choose to change behaviors or actions that affect their relationships, or to choose to change their relationship status though they confess to being dissatisfied and unhappy. They are making choices nonetheless, and in so doing, locking patterns in place and cementing bonds that contribute to distress. I've seen other couples willing to examine behaviors, accept individual responsibility and choose to make changes, who report an increase in satisfaction and happiness almost immediately.

I have heard individuals describe that they choose not to pursue things they want by creating reasons why their desires may not be practical or possible; choose not to make certain changes because they believe they're just trapped in circumstances; choose to continue ineffective or destructive beliefs, behaviors and actions, despite evidence of poor results, simply because they've always chosen that path; choose to deny reality; choose to be taken advantage of or victimized; choose to rationalize addictions; and choose to blame others for how they feel and what they do.

I have also witnessed individuals, even as young as middle schoolers, choose to battle heroically against the hand they were dealt in life, including horrendous abuse, to reclaim their true selves and create their own futures; choose to make meaning out of devastating circumstances, including incurable illness; and choose to take full responsibility for the direction of their lives and their own happiness.

During the upheaval of midlife, I've considered and made many choices that have had major consequences in my life – whether and how to commit to furthering my education; pursue a career change;

empower my kids; fight back against an unfair employer; rebound from divorce; enter new romantic relationships; re-evaluate and restructure current relationships; live on less; relocate to a new area; start over; and deal with loneliness among them.

Many of the choices have been stressful and excruciatingly difficult; however, I appreciate my ability and freedom to make choices. Usually I have chosen to do *something* instead of *nothing*, chosen to take an action rather than punt. I also have had opportunities to choose my feelings, which can range broadly along a spectrum: optimism vs. pessimism; hopefulness vs. sadness; confidence vs. fearfulness; contentedness vs. dissatisfaction; trust vs. doubt; vitality vs. loneliness. Those choices affect my emotions and happiness with my life every day, and thus my effectiveness, productivity and image I present to the world.

Choice is a muscle; without effective and contemplative use, it atrophies, becoming a mechanism to promote misery rather than a tool to amplify freedom. Choose it or lose it: The choice is yours, always and forever.

Compare In, Not Out: Man in the Mirror

In the substance abuse therapy group I co-led as an intern, the group leader would tell members to "compare in, not out" when he detected a member analyzing whose addiction was worse than another's, assessing who among members engaged in more risky or reckless behaviors or seeking salacious details about others' misfortunes and misadventures.

The leader's message to the addicts was as clear as the typical pre-school teacher's emphasizing individual responsibility and self-control to easily distracted children focused on others: "Worry about yourself."

It's a simple message, but one that takes discipline and introspection to implement, whether for the purpose of changing addictive behaviors or many other goals or pursuits in life in which the temptation is to compare ourselves to the status, abilities and accomplishments of others. The era of social media has compounded the phenomenon of "comparing out" through the instantaneous access we have into the windows of others' lives – their new jobs, kids' achievements, lively social gatherings, adventurous vacations and other things of which to be envious.

We would be more satisfied with our lives if we would "compare in, not out."

To me, "comparing in" means evaluating myself according to my assessment of my own potential, my ability to strive for and attain goals I believe are worth pursuing, being happy with what I have at any given time rather than desiring what I don't, and living life in a way that makes me feel positive about my actions, conduct and treatment of others, even though it will be far from perfect.

Still, living life without "comparing out" is a challenge for me, as I imagine it is for nearly everyone who hasn't mastered some form of meditation or inner peace. Right now, I am struggling against "comparing out" as I begin my second summer as a seasonal tennis instructor at a large beach resort tennis complex, a "gig economy" interlude as I make a career transition to counseling.

Among the instructors, several of whom are year-round employees, it is apparent I am low on the totem pole, just as I was last summer. I know what I have to do to be successful is to conduct each clinic and private lesson to the best of my ability, stay upbeat and high-energy, engage clients in a friendly and courteous manner, and work cooperatively with the staff as part of a team.

But I still find it hard to resist comparing the assignments and the number of on-court teaching hours I get – which determines income -- to others. Such "comparing out," and the ruminations it causes, only makes me feel worse; on the other hand, "comparing in" when I give my all for a lesson or clinic, or assist a fellow instructor when needed, makes me feel positive.

My career transition from public relations to counseling is another area where I have to fight the lure of "comparing out" and instead "compare in," basing my assessment on what I deem is fulfilling and achieves a sense of purpose.

Though there is potential for income growth with the establishment of an independent counseling practice in the future, my first job in the profession likely will pay me about half of what I was making in the public relations position I left. Eyeing the reality of my pending job search, it is challenging to avoid "comparing out" to other professionals in my age group who may be at the height of their earning potential and aren't worried about scraping by. That's when it's important to "compare in" and realize I chose this path for a reason and I am fully responsible for my decision and the outcome.

"Comparing in" is difficult because it puts the onus squarely on us for our own successes and failures, our current condition in life, our decisions and behaviors, and, perhaps most importantly, the way we feel about ourselves and our own satisfaction and happiness. When we compare ourselves only to our own standards, goals, morals, ethics and beliefs, we strip away self-delusions and rationalizations and are forced to see only the "Man in the Mirror," our only true compass.

The Fog of Mental Illness:
I Know There's Another Person
In There Somewhere

Of all the midlife tasks I've encountered, caring for my ailing mother was hands down the most difficult.

That includes two job layoffs; getting fired from another job after seven years because of a personal conflict with a boss; a dispiriting divorce; a career change necessitating a six-year slog through graduate school; and a devastating injury requiring more than a year of rehabilitation.

I use the term "caring" loosely. I'm not the greatest caregiver – at least that's what my first wife concluded.

I was the typical "sandwich" during midlife, raising kids while becoming a surrogate parent to my parent.

My mother tested my love, patience, tolerance and temper, down to my last nerve. And I have to acknowledge, when my mother was in her greatest times of need and was in her most depressed, ornery and bedeviling states, it was not me who truly was her prime caregiver and manager, it was my patient-as-a-saint second wife. I just tried – sometimes unsuccessfully – to follow her lead with an open heart and mind.

Now that my mother has died, I feel a little more freedom to tell a deeply personal family story, significantly abbreviated. I recognize most people wouldn't air their family's laundry, would keep it tight in the family, in the shadows. As a counselor, it's part of my job to bring mental illness out of the shadows, to reduce the stigma. My mother had mental illness.

Depression Takes its Toll

My mother's depression occurred during various stages of her life, manifesting later in her life as bipolar disorder, meaning she cycled between depression and manic, or hyper, behaviors. The combination of mental illness and accumulating physical ailments, including intractable rheumatoid arthritis, fueled each other, contributing to an unremitting downward spiral in my mother's final years and resulting in her sudden death from an undetermined cause at age 73.

Depression first hit my mother full force in her 30s, coinciding with her divorce. From my ages of 11 to 15, my mother suffered from several bouts of severe depression requiring a couple of months-long hospitalizations. When she was home as a single mother during that period, often she was barely functional, leaving my younger brother and me to largely fend for ourselves. There were times I was convinced she would die as a young woman, as her lack of appetite and insomnia caused her to wither away physically and treatment did not seem to work.

She eventually recovered later in my teen years, entered the workforce and went on to live a reasonably productive and stable life. She was a beautiful – but complicated (aren't we all?) -- person. She was a good friend to others, my number one supporter, and cared for me deeply. She wore her passions on her sleeve, such as politics. If not for her, I likely never would have run for political office, of course as a Democrat, the only party for her.

Childhood Demons

But she also carried demons from childhood that inhibited her life, and were amplified when her mental state was out of balance. Her parents were critical of her; she was never good enough, a "bad girl." Her self-esteem suffered, compounded by her feelings of shame because of her family and home's relatively impoverished condition. Her parents also were overly worried and fearful – neurotic, my mother would say – and as a result, over-protective. My mother responded in a positive way – by rebelling, asserting her independence, being stubborn, acting willfully, behaving in sneaky ways, including probably fibbing, to avoid her parents' disapproval, and satisfy herself.

While those traits likely served her well during a challenging childhood, I believe they may have made her harder to deal with in later adulthood when mental illness flared, though dealing with anyone with bipolar disorder can be a nightmare regardless of personality characteristics.

My mother had long periods of stability, stretching many years. But when in the grips of a bipolar episode, the illness was ferocious, grabbing hold of her like a rag doll and dragging her around at its whim. She was a wild card – we never knew what we would get from day to day.

During one manic episode, we had to literally restrain our mother from chasing police cars down streets in Washington, DC, so convinced she was that they were heading to Capitol Hill to intervene in a terrorist attack and she wanted to be part of the action. Without intervention, we were sure she would end up injured, abused, jailed or dead.

What many people don't understand about dealing with people with significant mental illness is how difficult it is to get the sufferer help. Hospitalization is strictly voluntary, except in cases where it is evident the person is a risk of harm to herself or others, a standard that is quite difficult to prove to law enforcement.

Mania

During my mother's two serious manic episodes in later adulthood, when her behavior was wildly erratic and mood swings drastic – essentially, like dealing with a person possessed by another being -- we struggled mightily to get her to voluntarily commit to hospitalization so she could be stabilized.

She resisted stubbornly for weeks on end, at times perversely turning those who loved her and were trying to help her into her enemies, behaving belligerently toward us and targeting us for biting comments, as if mental illness obliterated her filter and her subconscious assumed dominance.

She nearly torpedoed the sale of her house, a project on which her family had worked for months to get her into a better situation, where she would be safer physically, less isolated socially, and perhaps even receive care on site. She made the Realtor a target of her ire, as she did numerous medical and therapeutic professionals, out of frustration and distrust, believing they had consistently failed her or attempted to deceive her.

It was incidents and behaviors like these and more that caused my fuse to burn short and my temper to erupt more frequently than I like to admit. Even though I knew it was mental illness acting and talking, not my *real mom*, my frustration and despair at my seeming inability to influence a change or make a difference sometimes overwhelmed me and made me feel despondent and helpless. Counterproductively, I often relieved my anger by taking it out on my mother, feeling terrible afterward.

At the time she died – alone in her new apartment, with no one aware – she had come out of a manic phase and was stabilizing mentally and emotionally.

As much as she fought in later adulthood against receiving professional help and being hospitalized – surely the result of wretched hospitalization experiences in her 30s – I believe she realized deep down that she needed help, that she couldn't conquer the illness through sheer strength of will, that the people who cared about her had her best interests at heart. Because each time, after dragged out, emotionally exhausting battles, she did submit to voluntary hospitalization, and got better.

Unfortunately, her last go-round with the disorder must have taken a huge toll. She never got the chance to fully recover and get back to a normal life. We'll never know what impact her mental illness had on her ultimate physical demise.

Unfortunately for me, my memories of my mother are clouded by that final intense, dramatic chapter, by the veil of mental illness shrouding the real person, when, try as I might have to be forgiving, accepting, patient and understanding, I was not always on my best behavior and didn't always hold my tongue, just like my mother. And, perhaps worst of all, I never had the chance to apologize, forgive or say goodbye.

You're Gay? No Therapy for You!

A law enacted in 2016 by the Tennessee legislature affecting the counseling profession shows how some politicians simply are jackasses pursuing their own myopic, discriminatory agenda.

My 2016 book, *Don't Knock, He's Dead: A Longshot Candidate Gets Schooled in the Unseemly Underbelly of American Campaign Politics,* details some of the more repulsive and corrupt aspects of politics and those who practice the art. But the Tennessee law strikes close to home, as I am in the process of completing a graduate degree and clinical internships in counseling and becoming a mental health therapist.

Tennessee politicians passed a law allowing mental health counselors to decline to treat any client if counseling that client involves "goals, outcomes or behaviors that conflict with the sincerely held principles of the counselor."

This law's not-so-subtle aim is to allow counselors to discriminate against clients who identify as lesbian, gay, bisexual or transgender (LGBT), an attempt to strike back against gains won through the legal system recently for gay marriage and equal treatment. The so-called "sincerely held principles" law also would allow counselors to deny services to clients for any number of discriminatory reasons, such as if counselors disagreed with principles of Jews or Muslims, or with principles of cohabitating unmarried couples. Essentially, the law is codifying discrimination.

The law is in direct opposition to the American Counseling Association Code of Ethics, which states that counselors must avoid imposing their own values, attitudes, beliefs and behaviors on clients. In other words, the Code of Ethics forbids counselors from turning away clients who may be gay because they have certain attitudes or beliefs about gay people or the gay lifestyle.

Why Tennessee politicians felt they had to meddle in a self-regulating profession that is functioning well on its own is baffling, and demonstrates that many politicians are out-and-out jackasses using their office to impose their own narrow views on the populace. The American Counseling Association and the Tennessee Counseling Association vehemently opposed the law, yet politicians with little knowledge of the counseling profession and the profession's ethics saw fit to ignore the experts in the field.

Could you imagine if a legislature passed the same kind of law in opposition to the medical profession's ethics, allowing doctors to decline to treat gay people based on "sincerely held principles?" An emergency room doctor knows a patient rushed to the hospital is gay, and just passes on treatment?

Or the nurse's code of ethics? How about police? A police officer has a belief in opposition to gay people, so decides not to protect and serve during an assault because of that principle?

It should be no different for the counseling profession. And any counselor who declines to provide services to gay people has no business being in counseling. Hold onto your beliefs, values and religion, but get out of counseling, because your attitudes and discriminatory behavior don't belong. Counseling must. be one place where people who are gay – or people from any other social or religious group -- are accepted without discrimination or judgement, not another place where they will be rejected for who they are.

I am disgusted by Tennessee's law and the complicity of a majority of the state's lawmakers and its governor who promulgated it to promote their own brand of hate and unfounded fear of people who are "different." Jackasses, all.

I stand firmly behind the American Counseling Association and its Tennessee affiliate in all efforts to get this law repealed and show other states, some of which are following suit, that such discriminatory legislation will not stand. The ACA already has taken one bold action to show that counselors do not accept the blind and narrow-minded stupidity of legislators by pulling its 2017 national conference out of Nashville, TN, striking a blow to the state's economy and sending a message. More strong messages are in order.

A Walk in the Woods

Sometimes there's no better elixir than the woods. Tough week at work? Traverse a path. Relationship problems? Hike a hill. The winter blues? Trek along a river.

Or even when you don't feel distressed by anything, a walk in the woods can uplift your mood.

I've recently had a lot on my mind, having just made a major life change by moving in midlife to a new place away from friends and family and starting a new job in a new career. My life is in transition. So last week, I went to explore a really big wood in my adopted home state of South Carolina – the 260,000-acre Frances Marion National Forest.

At the outset of my hike, I did what I am wont to do: ruminated over things that are constantly on my mind, despite my desire to tame the gremlins while in the presence of natural beauty. I know I'm not alone in engaging in over-active self-talk – we all have ongoing conversations in our own heads at some volume – but I would like to tell my voice to just chill out sometimes.

The wood worked its magic. About 30 minutes and two wrong turns into my hike along a 7-mile trail, my self-conversation quieted, I stopped looking at my watch and I began observing – tall stands of forest pines and expansive views of marshlands along the Intracoastal Waterway. I realized I wasn't in a rush; I could walk as long as I wanted.

Time became irrelevant; I relinquished the nearly constant need to be on the clock.

I completed the last two hours of my walk with relatively few conscious thoughts other than what I was experiencing in the moment. It was rejuvenating to be free from intrusive thoughts. By the time I finished, I felt great – relaxed, gratified, naturally euphoric, tired in a good way.

In my counseling, I have often counseled clients who are experiencing symptoms of depression or anxiety to take a walk in the woods, whether it's a 30-mile-wide national forest or a trail along an urban stream. The acts of using one's senses in nature, spending time in daylight and sunlight and being physically active and energized can have healing effects mentally and emotionally. Make those acts a habit, and symptoms can be reduced.

Before I moved, a friend and I, along with his dog, had made a regular practice of riding bikes on a trail along the Patapsco River in Maryland. My friend would marvel at the beauty of the winding river and the hills rising from it, the rocks embedded in the hills and the impressive construction of the century-plus-old railroad tunnels. The ritual would be fully realized if a train ran by while we were resting by the tracks, so we could be awed by its length and wonder what freight it was carrying.

That trail became a sacred place for me and my friend. As I finished my walk in the woods, I thought about my friend and how he would like trekking this forest, and about the incomparable value of a sacred place where time slows down and your head clears up.

Tennis Teaching and Counseling: Immersion in "The People Business"

In summer 2016, I made the seemingly stark transition from working as a counseling intern in an outpatient mental health clinic serving low-income clients to teaching tennis at a large beach resort . One would think the two jobs would have nothing in common, both in clientele and job requirements, but that's not the case. What's the common denominator? Quickly evaluating, working with, and constantly interacting with people and all their personality types, moods, behaviors, idiosyncrasies and expectations.

In my previous job and career in public relations, I could frequently go a whole day with minimal direct interactions with people, if I wanted to. People in those jobs often interact mostly through their computer and e-mail and may even intentionally avoid personal, face-to-face conversations.

But that's not possible as a counselor or as a tennis professional. Tennis is a form of therapy for many people, a way to escape stress, immerse in a physical activity and release tensions on the ball and endorphins in the body. The tennis pro is the counselor on the court. Part of the pro's job is to figure out what makes people tick, what they want, how to engage, encourage and motivate them, and how to make them feel good about themselves.

And that's just referring to the paying clients. At the resort, there's a large staff of tennis teachers and administrative workers, all with their own personality quirks, with whom I must interact personally every day.

I've learned there's also some personality diagnosing taking place on the court, and learning how to interact with people differently. Some players are easy going and just happy to be playing; others are more demanding and have certain expectations – in other words, more difficult to please and more apt to complain or emphasize the negative. Many are happy; others crabby. Many are classic high-achievers; some are overly self-critical. Some players are filled with doubts while others have over-inflated egos. Some players like to talk a lot; others rarely utter a word.

Most parents are charming, but a few can be insufferable, as most tennis pros can attest. Most kids are a joy and are eager to please, while a few find pleasure in defiance and pushing limits. Some kids are more fragile than others. A few kids have emotional or behavioral challenges that present on the court.

While I doubt I will have any significant impact on anybody's life this summer in my role as a tennis pro, like I felt I did as a counseling intern, I believe I am getting great practice at interacting with strangers and seeking to get a sense of who they are and making a quick connection, skills that translate directly to the counseling environment and relationship.

I never thought these two seemingly disparate professions would have such similarities until I became immersed in the tennis resort environment. In many ways, it has been just as challenging as counseling because of the need to develop fast interpersonal relationships, with both my fellow teaching pros and clients. For an introvert like me, that is a skill I am going to be constantly honing, on the court or in a counseling session. In each profession, I am in "the people business."

CHAPTER 9

Substance Abuse and Recovery

'Play the Whole Tape:'
The Struggle of Addiction

The lanky young man with the tattoos took a break from his intricately-detailed pencil-sketching to look up from his art and turned to face me after I introduced myself to the group.

"Have you ever been addicted to drugs?" he asked.

"No," I responded.

"Ever been addicted to alcohol?"

"No," I said again.

"What can you know?" he mumbled with disgust and turned back to focus on his artwork.

It was my first day as a co-leader of a substance abuse therapy group, an internship for my clinical mental health counseling master's degree as I make a career transition from public relations to counseling. The group leader smoothed the edges by telling the group members they can learn different things from counselors who had addiction problems and those who haven't.

The leaders with whom I have worked had substance abuse histories and can talk the language of the streets and drug culture; I can't. When a member glorifies the days of using, as those in substance abuse recovery are wont to do, one leader admonishes: "Play the whole tape," meaning remember the misery that accompanied the action, the "ripping and running."

Later in the session, the young man apologized to me and the group for his abrasiveness, saying he had discovered just before the session that a good friend from childhood had died by drug overdose. That type of emotional volatility and chaotic, unpredictable life is common among members.

In my two months co-leading and leading this three-hour-long group session, I have learned from members and have become more comfortable guiding and interacting with them. The members provide a fascinating window on life's struggles and many life themes: redemption, commitment, determination, acceptance, grace, hope, resilience, courage, meaning, generosity, self-centeredness, self-destruction, temptation and despair.

Group members represent a microcosm of society: male and female; fathers and mothers; black, white and Hispanic; teenagers to seniors; those from childhoods of abuse, neglect and deprivation and others from relatively stable, caring families; workers and jobless; people doggedly seeking change and others going through the motions.

Some have been homeless, shunned by family members. Many have been imprisoned, and some still are dealing with charges that could result in jail time with any transgression. Some have risked their lives to get drugs, running dangerous streets at all hours, banging on doors of drug dealers. They have lost children, jobs, health, relationships, dignity, trust and respect over their addictions. Many have been through rehab before, but reverted to previous habits, some as soon as they exited. Their emotional lives have been engulfed with fear, shame, guilt, resentment, anger and damaged self-worth.

I don't have any particular unique or profound insight into the scourge of addictive behavior and those who come under the influence of alcohol and drugs. I only have impressions as a person and professional new and fairly oblivious to this world. My biggest takeaway is that these individuals are not addicts, but people with addictions. In our society, we tend to apply labels to people that come with proscribed traits and characteristics, effectively straight-jacketing people into circumscribed boxes.

The experience has reinforced for me that addiction does not define the group members, a lesson I also learned first-hand when a roommate suffered a relapse. In fact, addiction is not at the core of their being at all. They are so much more than "addicts." I appreciate the regular group members I have gotten to know for their sense of humor, loyalty, caring, openness, friendliness, raw honesty, suffering and commitment.

One woman exemplified the power of passion, hope and resilience – and the difference between those who truly accept and want to beat addiction and others who may be biding time – in an activity I led challenging the members to identify their strengths. Some struggled to come up with more than two; a few others declined to offer even one when called upon to share.

But this woman, for whom the phrase "to hell and back" would apply, rattled off about a dozen assets. She appears to want recovery bad; her emotional pain is palpable. She has a medical condition that might keep others away, but she refuses to miss or give up. She's a good person who got some raw deals in life and made some regrettable choices that sent her into a downward spiral, like many of the members, and she's developing the courage to own it all. She is recognizing her worth as a human. She expresses faith.

I'm pulling and praying for her and the others to beat their addictions and find serenity and contentment, and hope I can be a positive influence, however small, on their recovery.

A Different Type of Lunch Meeting

I attended my first Alcoholics Anonymous meeting on Friday, Jan. 23, 2015. But I'm not an alcoholic. Really, I'm not. I can take it or leave it. I can stop anytime. What's the problem? I know, I know, this is what all alcoholics say. But really, I'm not. Thank God.

I attended an AA meeting for my Loyola University counseling program class on Substance Abuse and Addictive Behaviors. Though I'm not an alcoholic, I've experienced family alcoholism, living between the ages of 14 to 18 with my father's live-in mate who had a drinking problem. I've never sought counseling or support to explore how living with an alcoholic affected my life and family relationships. The AA meeting motivated me to consider doing that.

At the AA meeting, I was stunned as I walked in the door and blown away by an incredibly humbling, uplifting, honest, heartfelt, connective and redemptive experience, all within an hour's time while the outside world was downing a sandwich for lunch. The participants carry a heavy burden, but also hold a treasure that few experience in a lifetime – a true connection to a community that has the depth, authenticity and spirituality that few relationships possess, and that I would contend is rare even in churches and other religious gatherings.

I found an AA meeting at a church within walking distance of my workplace, so attended a "Just Before Noon" session during my lunch hour.

The previous day in class, I had asked my professor how we could know if meetings listed on websites really took place as frequently as advertised, because I couldn't believe meetings would really be taking place several weekdays per week in the middle of the day at the same place. The professor responded that online listings could be hit-or-miss. But after class, a student who had been to meetings assured me that if a meeting was listed, people would be there, and to just look for a group of people smoking outside to know it was happening.

I tried to enter the church through the front doors. Locked. A lady approached and asked what I was looking for. I responded, "A meeting," and went to try the side door. Locked also. I was thinking my suspicions were confirmed – these meetings are probably sporadically attended, erratic and unreliable.

Then the lady pointed me to an adjacent building, a house converted into a church annex. That's when I was stunned. The room was teeming with people, filling coffee cups, chatting and embracing like old friends. I was expecting five or six attendees max, if I was lucky, and already had been making tentative plans to find another seemingly bigger meeting – perhaps something at night -- in case this one didn't provide the fodder I would need to write a five-page reflection and theory interpretation paper.

Sixty people or more filled a room with an inner horseshoe table and outer seated audience, the 12 steps unfurled banner-style at the front. There was a lot of gray hair and wrinkles – many attendees were older and wizened. Some had spent as many years as a hard drinker as a teetotaler; one dapper man, dressed finer than all the others in a burgundy sport jacket and tie, told the group he was just two years short of spending the same amount of years as a teetotaler than as a drinker: 34.

But by no means was it strictly an over-the-hill crowd; there was a sizable contingent in their 20s, 30s and 40s. About 40 percent were women, same wide age range.

Another elder statesman celebrating his 44th year of sobriety, wearing a furry hunting hat over a mane of white hair, was introduced to cheers, came to the front of the room, and told an impromptu, 20-minute, somewhat rambling, disjointed and humorous version of his life story, including being sent away to school as a third-grader by his alcoholic mother, a top-secret job involving an Air Force base and eventually, accompanying his mother to an AA meeting, something he thought he didn't need until he knew he needed it and couldn't live without. He also talked about the shirt he wore, a "flannel shirt, buttoned all the way up," which carried symbolism he learned from an AA mentor or AA tradition, but I wasn't sure exactly what it meant.

I'm guessing the flannel is for humility and hard work, rather than something like silk, and buttoned up signals no room for slacking or loosening up.

After Flannel's powerful story, the floor was opened for anyone who felt moved to speak about their struggles, sobriety, temptations, fears, insights and triumphs. Introductions always took the form of "Hi, I'm

Fred, and I'm an alcoholic" – whether sobriety had been for one month or 30 years – with the audience responding heartily, "Hi Fred!"

Stories from Inside the Bottle

In 30 minutes, I heard so many stories of despair, faith, hope, grace and spirituality that I felt completely immersed, thoughts of work assignments, weekend plans and anything else falling away. There were confessions of near-suicides, slides into homelessness and self-absorbed stupors. Several confessed that they "didn't know how to live" before becoming sober. They talked about acceptance of the self and giving up "striving for perfection" in their spiritual walk, realizing it was impossible, and surrendering to God, whatever He meant to each individual, as long as it wasn't a bottle. They cautioned against attending AA merely "to comply on paper" – orders from the legal system – because even if compliance was checked off, they would fall. The woman sitting next to me added her own commentary to herself whenever a revelation hit a chord.

One man told about getting drunk on vodka before attending a court-mandated Mothers Against Drunk Driving meeting at a courthouse, where, to his surprise, police were present, and detected his drunkenness. He could not be charged, but a judge paraded him in front of an audience of defendants as a shameful example.

A woman professed her love for everyone she had met in the group – well, 90 percent, she clarified – and how terrified she was that she would be leaving them shortly to move to Texas, but had already found an AA group there upon a good recommendation. A large, powerful-looking man confessed his abject weakness, describing how he went to his pastor at this very church to say he was "out of control" and needed help, and how he was guided next-door.

This man gave out the "chips" at the end of the meeting, signifying various anniversaries of time for sobriety. Each person who hit a milestone earned rousing applause upon collecting their chip. The shortest length was three weeks.

I left the meeting into the winter sunshine and walked through the adjoining neighborhood, back to my regular life. It struck me how oblivious I was that this spiritual revival of sorts was happening every Friday here and hundreds of other places around the country, and how I probably encountered participants in my everyday life, like my fellow Loyola student who gave me advice in class.

My Experience with Family Alcoholism

As for my own experience with alcoholism, I did not know my "Surrogate Step-Mother" was an alcoholic until I had already left for college, and she called me one day to tell me about her acknowledgement and new journey and to apologize. She was a high-functioning, covert alcoholic, not a raging drunk. I knew she liked to have a glass of wine in the evening, but that's all I knew. She could be irritable, moody, temperamental and rigid. She was an ambitious, driven, presumably hard-working professional. Who knows where and when she drank, and how clever she must have become at hiding it. To this day, I still don't know what my father knew or suspected, or when. We've really never talked about it. Not long after Surrogate told me about her alcoholism, she and my father broke up. I have never seen her since.

That has left me with unresolved questions about alcoholism. This was a woman I lived with for four years during my formative adolescence, and knew several years prior. Did her alcoholism make her want to escape from everything and everyone she knew during her alcoholic life? Why did she disappear? Shame and regret? A desperate need to start anew? Did this explain the reason for all the turmoil in our cobbled-together family system, the kids vs. the "parents" bunker mentality we adopted? How did it affect my father?

It took a class assignment 30 years later to make me even think about exploring these dynamics, but now I think I will.

Drunken Debacles

Ed's Chicken & Crabs, referred to by my family as Ed's Chicken Shack, a landmark in laid-back, party-hard Dewey Beach, DE for nearly 40 years where you could order consummate beach dinners of crabs, chicken, fried clams, hush puppies and corn on the cob from the take-out window and eat on picnic benches outside as the sun set, was reduced to a pile of charred wood and scorched, twisted metal in a fire this summer.

The fire wasn't caused by a kitchen or grease mishap. Neither was it caused by an arsonist, a careless smoker or an electrical misfiring. Unbelievably, it was caused by a drunken motorist at 2 a.m. who crossed the raised road median on Dewey's main drag and *four lanes of traffic* and slammed into a propane line in the eatery, igniting the blaze.

Luckily, the 36-year-old woman's life was saved by first responders. The owner of Ed's and its devoted Dewey Beach patrons weren't as lucky. Ed is 83 years old and said he doesn't plan to rebuild. A drunken woman put him out of business and left an eyesore of rubble in the middle of the classically honky-tonk beach town.

A beach institution is destroyed and a man's livelihood and surely a piece of his soul wrecked by a brazen act of drunkenness committed by someone of an age where one would hope maturity and individual responsibility would triumph over atrociously bad judgment and decision-making.

But that is not always the case when alcohol is involved, as Baltimoreans witnessed in the death of cyclist Tom Palermo, run over on a sunny afternoon by a drunken, high-ranking clergy member.

Speaking of drunken debacles, I experienced first-hand observation of a rapid descent into the throes of alcoholism during my summer teaching tennis in Bethany Beach, DE. An adverse life event pushed someone I was close to and saw on a daily basis straight inside a vodka bottle for a multi-week, nonstop bender. I had never seen alcoholism so up-close and devastatingly real before.

The fall was incredibly rapid and far by someone who claimed to have been sober for three years. In the course of a few days of drinking, I could barely recognize this person from the one I knew previously, sober. It was a stunning and sad transformation, and no one could do anything about it but the drinker.

A recovering alcoholic who knew both of us counseled me about what I could expect from my friend. Don't believe anything my friend said and expect the friend to do things in secrecy out of shame, the sober recovering alcoholic told me. Expect the plunge to go deeper and deeper until my friend ends up in the hospital or in jail, he said. That nearly did happen – my friend hurt himself physically on multiple occasions, got himself kicked out of bars, and had to be picked up on roadsides.

Finally, the recovering alcoholic advised, don't expect my friend to be able to pull out of the drunken stupor by sheer force of willpower. That display of personal strength against the pull of alcohol rarely, if ever, happens, he counseled. He knew from experience, that of himself and many friends and acquaintances he had met through his own journey to recovery. The first step, he said, is the alcoholic realizing he needs help, wanting help, and being ready to seek help. Detox, professional help and support is necessary for recovery. And that can't happen until the lies to self and others stop, he said.

I tried to offer my friend help as much as I could. But, as the recovering alcoholic advised, you can't force an alcoholic to accept help, you can only offer, and often my friend did not take me up on my offer to seek the help he needed.

Sometimes I sought to help, but in the wrong way. Like the time when my friend, who did not have a car, wrecked his bike and messed up the chain. My friend was desperately trying to fix the chain at 11 p.m. and asked for my assistance. Why the obsession to fix the chain so late at night? The bike was his only source of transportation and a necessary component for refueling his booze binge.

Eventually, both of us went our separate ways. We were each there only for the summer, like so many people who are employed in a beach town. My friend got his act together enough to leave town for his next stop.

But like many alcoholics, he was overwhelmed by all logistics and decisions.

I don't know yet if he was able to pull himself out of the bottle through sheer force of his will – against the odds, as the recovering alcoholic explained to me – and get back on a good track for his life. I truly hope so, or if not, that he got the help he needs. He will always be my friend for the experiences we shared together, good and bad, and I will always remember him for those same reasons, whether our paths cross again or not. I learned a lot from him – not just about alcoholism, which is important knowledge in the line of work I'm entering, counseling, but many other things of positive value.

I wish my friend safety, health, sobriety and Godspeed – freedom from the devastating effects and ruined relationships caused by alcohol. He will always be my friend – a good, well-meaning and caring person at heart who also happens to have an alcohol problem over which he must be constantly vigilant.

A Tragic Tale of Alcoholism

Alcoholism is an insidious disease. Those with the hubris or self-delusional thinking to believe they can confront it and defeat it or manage it without professional help and community support, or who are oblivious, willfully or otherwise, toward recognizing their problem, invariably lose. That's not to say that people with alcoholism who choose to go it alone are senseless, just that they are human and flawed, and as such, stubborn, prideful, in denial, and resistant to surrender. This is the tragic story of one of them.

Names have been changed.

I received a text message overnight from Monty*, the head tennis pro at a community recreation center near where I was teaching tennis for the summer at a seaside resort. We had met early in the vacation season to talk about whether he had need for assistance and whether I could work around my schedule to teach at his club.

As a last-minute replacement hire, Monty also struggled to find housing for his three-month gig, which is prohibitively expensive and scarce at the shore. So throughout the summer, it was common for him to text me to help him with his housing search or to let me know his teenage assistant wasn't working out and to ask whether I had any availability to teach.

But this text was different. It was shocking, but unfortunately, not entirely surprising:

"Adam, I heard your friend Kevin is no longer with us. If it's true, I'm sorry for your loss."*

I didn't see the text until the morning, just before I started teaching for the day. When I got home, I searched online to see if I could find any confirmation of what Monty had relayed to me. I did. It was a sad, bizarre and surreal article in a Caribbean newspaper, but rang true to what I knew about my friend Kevin. Alcohol did him in.

The article described how Kevin had traveled to the Caribbean island from the U.S. Heartland in hopes of securing a tennis teaching job at an island resort. In unusually detailed reporting, the article also explained that Kevin was unable to land a job because he remained drunk all day and night, and had numerous cuts stitched up on his head from falls as testament to his non-stop drinking. According to the article, Kevin drowned in shallow waters beneath a coastal town's popular boardwalk, lined with restaurants and bars. By the time passers-by spotted him and pulled him out, he was gone. He was 61.

The Odd Couple

Kevin and I not only were roommates for summer 2016, but taught tennis alongside each other at the large coastal resort. We spent more time together than a married couple, especially since Kevin did not have a car.

He said his car had some mechanical problems and that he did not want to take it on the long trip from the Midwest to the Atlantic shore. I took him at his word at the time, but now I suspect he might have lost his license due to drinking-related violations. It might have been one of those little lies he told others and himself to mask an unpleasant truth.

I took him on shopping and banking errands, restaurant outings and side trips, and we usually drove to work together, with his bike on the back of my car in case our departure times were different. He called me his "wing man" on social outings. We shared lunch breaks at the tennis center and barbeque dinners at home. When it rained, we sometimes taught side-by-side on the same indoor court.

Together, we watched his favorite Midwestern teams compete in the NBA Playoffs and hockey's Stanley Cup at restaurants until our cable TV got hooked up, then from our couch.

When I first made Kevin's acquaintance by phone, I got the impression that Kevin, at age 60, was mellow and wise, a sage who would bring harmony to any situation. While that impression wasn't entirely inaccurate, it missed the mark.

From the moment I met Kevin on my first day at the tennis resort, when he burst through the clubhouse doors sweaty and pepped up from his bike ride to the facility, and zeroed in on me immediately as his new roommate, colleague and man he had communicated with by phone and email for several months, I knew he was more like the proverbial "real pistol," a whirling dervish, belying his near-senior citizen status.

We were The Odd Couple – he the big-talking extrovert prone to braggadocio, the raconteur of uproarious stories, the unabashedly gutter-mouthed chatterer, the lifelong bachelor, the conqueror of beautiful women, the bon vivant, the energetic go-getter, the confident expert in his field; me the introvert, the married man with kids, the calm and contemplative one, the boring one satisfied to do solitary things at home and rest, the relative newbie at big-time tennis teaching who didn't know if he fit correctly within the zeitgeist of the profession. But somehow, the yin and yang worked; we played off each other like Felix and Oscar.

I've Got to Get out of this Place

Kevin – who introduced himself as "Coach Kev," the same as he was called by his students -- got in touch with me in spring 2016, several months before we both showed up in the beach town as seasonal tennis instructors, to make my acquaintance and discuss strategies for searching for a place to live for the summer. We talked numerous times about our backgrounds and experiences, and our prospects for securing housing.

In the course of those discussions, Kevin revealed that he was an alcoholic, had attended Alcoholics Anonymous, had a sponsor, and had been sober for three years. He said he had been sidetracked from his tennis teaching and coaching career by an illness and death in his family, forcing him to return to his Midwestern hometown after globetrotting for two decades, bouncing around among eight states from the Southeast to the Mid-Atlantic to the Midwest to the Northeast, with an interlude in China.

In hindsight, I suspect that transient existence may have had something to do with Kevin's battles with alcohol.

He was eager to get away from what he called his "gloomy" Midwestern home state and a grunt-labor factory job he worked while caring for his family member to "build a nest egg" to jump-start a better life doing what he loved. The tennis court was his sanctuary.

"Can't wait to get out of here and to the beach!!!" he wrote in one email.

"Let's work hard and have some fun and learn something about each other and the rest of the team this summer," he wrote in another.

Fish Tales

I secured a room for rent in a homeowner's house two miles inland from the beach, and connected Kevin with the homeowner Steve*, who rented Kevin the other available room.

The three of us became friends during the summer of 2016, engaging in fraternity-like banter about each other's social lives, eating and shopping habits, athletic prowess, and quirks. Kevin told stories about living with a trio of Swedish girls while working in a ski resort town and adventures in Alaska, where he claimed to be a friend of singer Jewel. We all laughed at Kevin and Steve's evening rituals of lawbreaking, when they would walk through neighbors' property to fish in the adjoining private golf course's pond and play the closest three holes as freeloading non-members, both activities prohibited.

Steve and I cracked up as Steve recounted Kevin's reaction when admonished by a golf course superintendent that fishing was not allowed on the golf course.

"What do you MEAN there's no fishing?!" Kevin bellowed incredulously to the golf course official, fishing line dangling in the water from the bank, as if those golf course fish were Kevin's God-given right to catch.

I still have the hilarious image in mind of Kevin striding purposefully down our neighborhood street, wearing his floppy fishing hat and fishing vest with dangling lures and hooks, wading pants and boots, fishing pole carried erect, looking comically out of place amid the trailers and modular homes with no river or lake within proximity. Invariably, he would come home in darkness with a fishing tall tale, immediately pulling out his cell phone to show me photos of and describe in vivid detail his evening's triumphs.

The Big Dog

On the tennis court, Kevin was intense and driven – perhaps too much so for a resort environment. He had a strong desire to demonstrate his knowledge and skill, and seemingly to show he was superior to other tennis coaches, The Big Dog, which appeared true but may have rubbed some the wrong way.

He sometimes became frustrated with lackadaisical players on his court during clinics, urging them, "Move, players, move!" Some liked to be pushed;

others felt browbeaten – after all, they were on vacation, not training for Wimbledon. On occasion, when players failed to listen or couldn't understand instructions, Kevin would turn his back to players and perform the religious ritual of crossing his chest and looking toward the heavens in mock – or in his case, perhaps all too real -- despair.

Kevin was an excellent tennis coach, with a knack for explaining technique, strategy, shot selection and court positioning in simple, succinct and understandable terms. Players who were truly interested in improving their games gravitated to him, booking private lessons. Parents who wanted to help their kids compete at a higher level often sought out Kevin to be their coach for a week or two, or intermittently during the summer, deeming him the instructor who could produce the most results.

I learned a lot from Kevin about tennis coaching and teaching. I often watched his lessons and took notes on his sayings, advice, instructions and drills. Invariably, Kevin would bring his day at work home with him, recounting each teaching hour of his day, analyzing individual players on his court and their idiosyncrasies, describing what went well and what didn't, and sharing his observations of other coaches, administrative staff and the entire tennis resort operations. He assumed the role of self-appointed management consultant and evaluator, seemingly unsatisfied to limit himself to his more narrow daily duties.

He would ask me about each of my clinic hours and students, and offer commentary on what he observed of my on-court performance. We often engaged in hours-long discussions on the finer points of tennis stroke production, doubles strategy and movement, ball-feeding patterns, purposeful drills, and how to keep clinics fast-paced, engaging and informative. He used his fingers to diagram and explain drills on our kitchen counter, moving them along the Formica® to demonstrate the flow.

His intensity and high standards often extended to the tennis club's administrative staff, which caused him anguish when he believed they were lax or did not communicate well, especially about scheduling and booking issues.

"They're taking money out of my pocket," was Kevin's frequent refrain.

As a result, tensions mounted between some of the young desk assistants, who may have felt intimidated or unfairly criticized, and Kevin, who expected a high level of professionalism. His reasonable but firmly delivered demands for accountability may have hurt him in the end.

Kevin was full of bluster and confidence. Even though he was 60, he approached the tennis teaching gig like he was 25, insisting with bravado that long hours on his feet in temperatures hovering around 90 were "a piece of cake." Recognizing his desire to work and customers' appreciation of his coaching skill, the club worked him hard. Some days, Kevin would start with an 8 a.m. lesson, and would finish with the 6 p.m.

evening clinic, arriving home by bike at 7:30. The grind finally wore on him. "They're riding me like a mule!" he would confess, sweaty and red-faced.

Voluntary and Involuntary Transitions

As the summer wore on, Kevin realized it was time for him to search for his next gig, as our tennis center dramatically cut its teaching staff after Labor Day. After several weeks of negotiations, Kevin proudly announced that he had secured a tennis teaching job at a large Florida facility. Kevin, who came from a family of eight siblings, called one of his brothers to share the good news, and became frustrated when he was met with skepticism and disapproval.

Late at night, after the phone call, he knocked on my bedroom door, wanting to talk. He lamented that his brother and other siblings didn't share his joy in nabbing the Florida job, but instead seemed to want him to head back to his Midwestern home base and hunker down with something more stable and secure. He assured his brother that he was doing well, was happy and sober, and was excited about the new opportunity.

Sad and reflective during our conversation, he seemed distraught by how difficult it had become to relate to close family members and their seeming lack of confidence in him and support for him, and needed an ear to bend. Coach Kevin was headstrong. He wasn't the kind to do what others wanted him to do with his life, and resented the insinuations that others knew what was best.

Soon after Kevin scored the new job and his distressing phone call, things began to unravel. I'm not sure if a slip from drinking abstinence precipitated trouble at our tennis club or trouble at the club precipitated drinking. As far as I could tell, Kevin had done a fantastic job staying sober, resisting temptations, grinding on the tennis court and keeping himself on track all summer.

But in August, Kevin was let go from his job. He received a call one morning, and left home early for work.

During busy morning clinic hours, when Kevin typically could be heard five courts away barking instructions and exhorting his players, Kevin was nowhere to be found.

At lunch, the tennis director and head pro pulled me aside, as a courtesy since I was Kevin's roommate, to let me know they had let him go that morning.

Relapse came fast and hard for Kevin, and with it, the ravages of alcoholism. Within a few days, his descent was so steep I couldn't even recognize the Kevin I knew, from confident, energetic, strong and outgoing to weak, bumbling, indecisive and lost. He was a shell of his former self. For several weeks after his firing, with nothing to occupy his time, Kevin's days revolved around drinking and were spent secretively in a drunken fog and the throes of violent physical illness, and in desperate but futile attempts to stop.

He knew he was sick and needed help, but refused to accept help from his roommates and a few other friends, always appreciating and thanking us for offers but never following through. He resisted regularly attending a nearby Alcoholics Anonymous meeting. He stubbornly persisted in his effort to slay the dragon on his own through sheer force of will, or maybe perversely preferring to wallow alone in misery as a form of self-punishment, shame and guilt.

He startlingly and rapidly declined physically, lacking sleep and nutrition and looking like he had been in a barroom brawl from numerous cuts on his head, hands and legs incurred from falls, similar to what was reported in the Caribbean newspaper about his final weeks.

With prompting and help from Steve, Kevin got his act together enough to pack some of his stuff, buy a bus ticket to Florida, and hitch a ride to the bus depot with Steve for departure. But I suspected in his condition, his new venture would be doomed from the start.

An Unexpected Reunion?

Kevin and I left messages for each other several times in the fall, but had difficulty connecting. In messages and short conversations, it wasn't clear exactly what he was doing, but I gathered that Florida had not worked out and he ended up back at his Heartland home base.

Then, in spring 2017, he contacted me to let me know he was making a comeback, literally. He was up for two seasonal tennis director jobs at a country club and the planned community recreation center along the same stretch of Mid-Atlantic shore that we both worked the previous summer.

He offered me to be his assistant during my off times at wherever he landed, knowing that I was returning to the bigger tennis resort at which we both had worked the previous summer as my main job. I said I was interested, but couldn't guarantee him anything, owing my allegiance contractually to my employer and working unpredictable schedules day-to-day.

He took the job at the community recreation center, keeping me updated on his programming plans and anticipated needs for an assistant pro. Once again itching to leave the gloomy Midwest behind, he arrived at the shore a good two months before the busy summer season began in earnest.

In one phone call before the summer season started, Kevin sounded particularly anxious and downbeat about his inability to find a reliable assistant, a lack of support and tennis industry knowledge on the part of the recreation center management, and the challenges of designing a schedule, implementing programs, establishing a budget and purchasing equipment. The responsibility all fell to him as a one-man operation, and he seemed to be feeling the pressure.

Downward Spiral

Within days, I got a call from Steve saying that Kevin had fallen off the wagon, had been hospitalized and had lost his tennis director's job, replaced in an emergency hire by Monty. He hadn't even made it to Memorial Day.

Kevin eventually caught a bus back home to the Midwest. I talked to him a couple of times while he was there. He told me ruefully that he "screwed up," that he was depressed and about to enter a 30-day rehab program, that if he didn't he feared he would die. But about a week later, I received a voice message from Kevin. In our previous conversation, he said he wouldn't be allowed to have a cell phone in rehab. I concluded he had decided not to attend rehab at all, or bailed or got kicked out after a few days.

I didn't hear from or about Kevin again for the rest of the summer, until I got the text late at night on September 1 from Monty, who had heard the news from the board president and manager of his recreation center/tennis club, where Kevin had preceded Monty as the short-lived tennis director.

In an odd and admittedly delusional way, I feel like maybe, just maybe, I could have changed the course of Kevin's life and saved him from his drunken stumble to his death off the gorgeous island's boardwalk. Maybe if I had been able to offer him more assurance that I could assist him in his new job at the shore, relieving some of his anxiety. Or perhaps if I had been in touch with him more frequently over the summer, providing him someone less judgmental than family members in whom to confide or vent fear and frustration.

But I know that is unrealistic, fooling myself about having any power or influence over the death grip of alcohol and its captive.

Without the alcoholic's full surrender to the indomitable potency of alcohol and to a power greater than oneself, bystanders can do little to save the alcoholic from himself. Lord knows, Kevin's many family members must have tried mightily to exert power or influence over the years, only to be rendered helpless in the end.

Nowhere to Escape

This is speculation, but my best guess is that Kevin had a tennis industry contact on the Caribbean island who encouraged him to relocate with the promise of leads for tennis teaching jobs. The newspaper article said Kevin stayed at a private residence on the island before moving into a hotel, a possible indication that drinking may have disrupted his stay with someone he knew.

Maybe Kevin wanted to make the ultimate escape, leaving behind the U.S. mainland, family, friends and acquaintances, and past job failures and bad memories, all together for a tropical paradise, where everybody is in good spirits, the slate is clean, and beauty abounds. Problem was, he couldn't escape himself and his disease. Ultimately, it appeared, he ended up in a place where nobody – or perhaps practically nobody -- knew him, where he could blend into the scenery and surrender, willfully or not, to his vice and disease unfettered, instead of to a higher power, without the watchful eye or emergency intervention of anybody who cared, a paradise that paradoxically turned ultimately into his own private hell.

I haven't been able to stop thinking about Coach Kevin since I heard the news and found the article. It doesn't seem real, but more like "fake news." I keep thinking that I will hear from him again, about his next stop in his series of adventures, and to check in on me. But his disease was all too real.

Though he could drive me a little nuts with his hyper-analysis of our tennis teaching days and critiques of my performance – often backing off later saying, "Ahh, don't listen to me…I'm just trying to help ya" – I appreciated Coach Kevin as a one-of-a-kind character. I've never met another Coach Kevin in my life – the intensity, the bravado, the humor, the sailor's mouth, the entertaining stories, the wide-ranging opinions, the passions, the insights, the hard-learned wisdom, the friendliness, the complexity of his personality and being.

He was one of those people you come across in life who you never forget, who makes an indelible impression. I was glad to call Coach Kevin my friend and I'll always remember him, even though we were so different and entered each other's lives late and for only a brief period.

I am deeply saddened by the loss of my friend. It would have been wonderful to keep in touch for years to come, sharing tales of new adventures and offering support and encouragement. The only solace is that Coach Kevin is free from the demon that he just could not tame despite what had to be many repeated Herculean, gut-wrenching efforts.

I imagine him looking down at me during my last few days teaching in the summer of 2017 and saying in his own inimitable, blunt-spoken way: "That lesson was miserable! What were you doing? I could have had that woman ripping topspin forehands into the corners in five minutes! Pow. Pow. Pow. Ahh, but don't listen to me..."

CHAPTER 10

Social, Cultural and Religious Observations

Minimalism: More Freedom, Less Crap – Material and Otherwise

Minimalism is a tool that can assist you in finding freedom. Freedom from fear. Freedom from worry. Freedom from overwhelm. Freedom from guilt. Freedom from depression. Freedom from the trappings of the consumer culture we've built our lives around... Minimalists search for happiness not through things, but through life itself.

The Minimalists, Joshua Fields Millburn and Ryan Nicodemus

In a medical office waiting room, I stumbled across a reference to a book that piqued my interest, *Everything That Remains*, a memoir by two Dayton, Ohio young men with working class upbringings and early adulthood, ladder-climbing, wealth-accumulating ambitions, about their gravitation from the timeworn path toward an illusory standard of The American

Dream to something more introspective and streamlined called Minimalism.

I found it at the library and read it. You might think the rest of this essay will be a screed about the evils and vacuousness of materialism and consumerism, and the beauty and simplicity of deprivation and Idealism, and a door-to-door-Bible-salesman-like proselytization aimed at convincing you to chuck the former's wanderings through a vast commercial wasteland in favor of a holier life spent in the latter's pure Garden of Eden. Breathe a sigh of relief; it won't be.

The book did put a name to the broad ideas about how I'd prefer to live, though. And I believe I'm largely putting those ideas into practice.

When people hear the term "Minimalism" applied to a lifestyle, it does seem to conjure the image of someone just barely better off than Fed Ex plane crash survivor Tom Hanks' character stranded on an uninhabited island in CASTAWAY, fashioning shoes from palm fronds, feverishly twirling a stick on a rock to start a fire, and squeezing meager marine nourishment out of a shellfish speared with a homespun, sharpened bamboo pole.

They think Minimalism means living a Spartan, monk-like, stripped-down existence: doing without, possessing no things, having no fun, staring at four bare walls from a lonely chair, living in a quixotic commune, scraping by on the minimum, spending no money – hell, MAKING NO MONEY! It doesn't.

What Minimalism means to me, as The Minimalists describe it, is eliminating the clutter from my life – figuratively and literally – so that all I have left and all that I focus my attention and physical, mental and emotional energy upon are things that add value and meaning to my life.

The Minimalists love the book/movie FIGHT CLUB, about an underground, subversive group of men breaking free from the soul-numbing shackles imposed by societal, cultural and corporate expectations, citing this quote from Fight Club's charismatic leader Tyler Durden: "The things you own end up owning you."

Eliminating oppressive, useless clutter that bogs you down applies to relationships, careers, meaningless pursuits and time-consuming obligations – real or imagined – as well as physical objects. That's the freedom to which The Minimalists refer.

Minimalism is about breaking free from corporate and cultural influences that tell you who you should be, how you should act, what you should believe and how you should define success. It's about the freedom to define your own path toward happiness and fulfillment, regardless of the disapproval and negativity you may receive from friends, family, colleagues and acquaintances. It's about the freedom to take risks, the freedom to make choices, the freedom to make mistakes and fail, and the freedom to take full responsibility for all of that in service of living a more courageous, authentic, satisfying and inspiring life.

It so happens that my recent movement toward Minimalism – a transition to a new career in mental health counseling from public relations, a move to a smaller area with a simpler lifestyle – has coincided with a more Spartan lifestyle, more out of necessity than by design. I have moved from a 3-bedroom, 4-bathroom townhouse to a 1-bed, 1-bath apartment. I am earning a salary that is less than half of my last full-time job salary, the result of the career change and starting on a bottom rung in a region with lower wages. I am not "livin' large" – I'm driving a 15-year-old economy car; watching the smallest-possible, decade-old flat-screen TV, donated to me by a friend, on a no-frills cable TV package; and sleeping on a real bed only after weeks on a constantly-deflating air mattress, because I had no bed to take on my move – but I'm livin' free and livin' well.

I have no debt, save for my mortgage, the house I moved from but still own, and which still adds value to my life. I feel a greater sense of meaning and purpose in my new career than my former, so much so that retirement holds no allure for me at age 54, which I consider a good thing. I am pursuing activities and relationships that enhance my life.

I am a proponent of Minimalism, not because I want to latch on to the latest fad or lifestyle trend that may be featured on the TODAY show or in chic lifestyle magazines, but because my re-evaluation of the course of my life during the reflective midlife phase was pointing me in the direction of Minimalism before I realized the philosophy had been assigned a pithy label. I am striving to be a Minimalist – not impoverished, deprived, lonely, isolated, rigid, overly austere, Utopian, cultist, weird, eccentric, anti-social, anti-consumerist, or anti-technologist (think Unabomber) – but free to embrace and fully pursue the things I value.

This quote from Minimalism's emblematic movie, *Fight Club*, captures the undercurrent stimulating the Ohio natives' cum Montana entrepreneurs' lifestyle movement:

"Man, I see in Fight Club the strongest and smartest men who've ever lived. I see all this potential, and I see squandering. Goddammit, an entire generation pumping gas, waiting tables—slaves with white collars. Advertising has us chasing cars and clothes, working jobs we hate so we can buy shit we don't need. We're the middle children of history, man: No purpose or place. We have no Great War. No Great Depression. Our Great War's a spiritual war; our Great Depression is our lives. We've all been raised on television to believe that one day we'd all be millionaires, and movie gods, and rock stars. But we won't. And we're slowly learning that fact. And we're very, very pissed off."

Baltimore Riots Hit Close to Home

The 2015 Baltimore riots in the wake of Freddie Gray's death while in police custody became personal. As disturbing as it was to see Baltimore looted and burned on television from my living room in my suburban community 20 miles away, it was still anonymous rioters wreaking havoc on anonymous victims. That changed.

I got an e-mail from my tennis community friends that a Korean-American who I have played against in tennis leagues, played with on the same team, and partnered with in doubles, was injured (I don't know how seriously) and lost his business, a liquor store, to rioters.

The e-mail said that my one-time doubles partner "was knocked out by a brick, kicked, punched, batted, and pick-pocketed," and that his wallet and cell phone were stolen. It continued: "His store was overrun by violent protestors who broke into his business, looted everything and eventually burned the store down. The store has since been boarded up by the Fire Department. Everything is lost. Everything is ruined."

The *Wall Street Journal* referred to my tennis partner's tragedy in its April 28, 2015 story: "Several other fires burned around the city, including at Fireside North, a liquor store in West Baltimore, where a resident said the owner had given all his cash to looters before pleading unsuccessfully with them not to burn his shop. The shaken owner declined to comment." Though the

WSJ didn't name the owner, a Korean online news organization did – it was my friend.

Overall, this is a tremendously complex situation that has played out in communities across the country that involves many factors including racism, police abuse of force, intergenerational poverty, lack of economic opportunity, failing educational systems, deplorable housing, the drug trade, lack of political will to address entrenched, systemic problems, hopelessness and isolation.

But what happened to my tennis partner is not complicated. It's criminal, pure and simple. And those who perpetrated the violence and destruction should be apprehended and brought to justice – just like the Baltimore police officers who were responsible for the treatment and death of Freddie Gray, if they are found through the legal process to be culpable.

In my graduate school class, Diversity Issues in Counseling, I read, "Black Like Me," a book by a white author who took dermatological drugs that darkened his skin so he could experience life as a black man in the U.S. South and write about his daily life, observations and experiences. John Howard Griffin's courageous experiment took place in 1959, a time of overt, oppressive and nearly intractable racism. But even 55 years later, one of his poignant observations still rings true, as demonstrated in Baltimore:

"I pray that the Negro will not miss his chance to rise to greatness, to build from the strength gained through his past suffering, and, above all, to rise beyond vengeance. If some spark does set the keg afire, it will be a senseless tragedy of ignorant against ignorant, injustice answering injustice – a holocaust that will drag down the innocent and right-thinking masses of human beings. Then we will all pay for not having cried for justice long ago."

Griffin was right. Economic and social justice have been too long denied by a society too willing to look the other way while those unfortunate enough to be born into depraved and oppressive inner city blight conditions suffer through no fault of their own.

But he also was dead-on about the need to "rise beyond vengeance," and about the "senseless tragedy" of "injustice answering injustice," dragging down innocent and well-intentioned people through base behavior that harms the brave actions of those who dare to "rise to greatness" and address injustices through civil methods exemplified by the likes of Martin Luther King Jr. and Mahatma Gandhi.

My tennis partner was an innocent who was dragged down by vengeance. I am angry at the City of Baltimore for that. I have no doubt that more could have and should have been done to protect him, and others who suffered similar losses at the hands of criminals exploiting a volatile situation. I hope he is able to recover physically and economically. Whether he would ever be able to recover trust in a community he served, and that shattered it – both the city's power structure and the criminals who attacked him and his livelihood – would seem less likely.

An Authentic Conversation

In 2015, I made my every-five-year pilgrimage driving to my 30th college reunion at Colgate University in the tiny upstate village of Hamilton, NY.

But this time, I had extra motivation: the opportunity to participate as an author in a book-signing event, my first public appearance to promote the self-published *Three Yards and a Plate of Mullet.*

Colgate is a beautiful campus in a picturesque setting, so I enjoy going back and seeing a small group of friends with whom I lived freshman year and with whom I participated on a particularly zealous intramural team through senior year.

But the vast majority of my classmates are strangers – some people I never knew at all, and others I may have known as acquaintances but certainly not anymore with the passage of time.

So I decided to try a social experiment during this reunion, especially since I was going there to be a self-promoter anyway. I would step out of my comfort zone and my small bubble of friends and introduce myself and talk to people from my class whom I didn't know well. I knew everyone would be doing the same thing – socializing and hanging with the same people they did 30 years ago, and for the most part overlooking others who weren't part of their group.

It's human nature. Cliques don't change. There's comfort in cliques, comfort in what's known. There's risk in stepping out. It's not easy for a person like me, an introvert by nature but who still likes to be sociable and can flip the extroversion switch at times. I just have to be in the right mood, or make a conscious effort to be more outgoing.

My social experiment went pretty well. I hung out with an old friend I had known since middle school and two of his college friends, who I had not known before. I sold one book on the spot just by introducing myself and talking with a classmate, who got out her cell phone and ordered from Amazon on the spot.

I talked with one drunk graduate 25 years my junior about his entrepreneurial idea to launch a business sales website, and a drunk nurse who turned out to be the daughter of the owner of a popular pub in the college town. I'm counting the drunkards even though they tend to babble on endlessly, just because I stuck with it long enough to learn about them.

But the most interesting conversation of the reunion weekend came out of the blue. I was hanging out with my new buddies in a side room where the soda dispenser was located during our class dinner, not feeling much like mingling in the main hall because I was enjoying the company of these guys. A woman walked in who I recognized. I had never known her well, but I knew we lived in the same dorm freshman year and must have had many mutual acquaintances from that time.

I introduced myself and we wound up talking by the soda machine for maybe five minutes. There was nothing spectacular about that. Anyone can chit-chat about the weather, where they live or their job for five minutes. What was exceptional about this conversation compared to any other I had at reunion was the depth of the content in a time so short that it would normally be reserved strictly for small talk.

She told me she was going through a divorce after about 20 years of marriage and three sons. I replied that I had experienced a similar situation, except with younger kids and a shorter marriage. I asked if she was the one who wanted the break or if it was mutual. She responded that she didn't want a divorce; it was at her husband's initiative. I said mine happened the same way. She acknowledged that divorce "sucks." I asked her how her sons were handling it. She responded that the two older ones seemed OK, but the youngest, a teenager, was having a hard time coping with it.

Then she told me what was weighing heavily on her mind as part of the divorce package: she was faced with selling her house and moving within a month or two. Again, I told her I had been through a similar scenario. I wished her the best in handling a difficult time of life. She knew I had participated in the author signing and expressed an interest in the book, so I took down her e-mail to correspond later.

And then we said goodbye and she left the room. I saw her again at breakfast the next morning, but from a distance and only long enough to wave hello. And that was that. I did e-mail her with information about *Three Yards and a Plate of Mullet* after I got home, but didn't hear back.

This woman invited me into the most consequential happenings in her personal life during a brief encounter. Why, I don't know. We could have just as easily talked about nothing for five minutes, or just said a quick hello and gone separate ways. I was grateful she engaged in a conversation with meaning. I got to know her – the real person with real life issues – just a little, and it felt genuine to make an authentic connection, as brief as it was. Such authentic conversations in which someone dares to reveal something personal and meaningful are all too rare, and makes life and personal interaction so much more lively and interesting.

Getting to Know My Muslim Neighbors

While driving near home, I passed a banner on the property of a Muslim mosque promoting an "Open House" later in the day. As a graduate student in counseling with courses in Diversity and Religious Perspectives as part of my program, I decided to visit to learn more about Islam directly from the source, especially amid the current national environment of fear, misinformation, rhetoric and propaganda about the religion that is based on the 1,400-year-old Qur'an.

I'm glad I did.

Non-Muslims came to talk to the mosque's Muslim "guides," ask questions and observe a prayer session. It was encouraging just to see the interaction and effort toward greater understanding at the Dar Al Taqwa mosque, which, translated, means "The Home of Consciousness" or "The Home of God-Fearing People." My "guide," a Baltimore pediatrician and Pakistan native, explained that Muslims pray five times daily, as a way to observe their belief that their God (Allah) sets the path and that their mission in life is to act as servants of God. Even during his medical training, he found the time and space he needed to observe his prayer ritual – it was that vital to his life.

My shoes left outside the sanctuary, I watched a group of about 35 males in a line, led by one man, in silent prayer for about 10 minutes, except for the brief utterances of the leader. The males alternately stood, bowed and kneeled with their heads near the floor. My guide later told me that the males were mentally reciting verses from the Qur'an.

After the prayer session, I asked my guide some probing and sensitive questions. Why were there no women praying with the men, I wondered. My guide explained that it was true that Muslim men and women were separated in some ways and roles in Islam, including in the ritual of prayer. However, separateness was not an indication of superiority or inferiority, the doctor said. American Muslim women have professional lives just like the men, and are relied upon to determine the future of their families and serve in other specific roles.

I asked his view of the typical American's lack of understanding of Islam. He responded that Muslims take it as a challenge to try to educate Americans of different religious backgrounds about the tenets of Islam, which he said can be described in three words: peace, love and service.

The reason the mosque holds open houses every few months is to dispel misconceptions through face-to-face meetings.

We discussed whether the doctor believes that Muslims are integrated into American life and viewed as contributors to society, acknowledging that some view Muslims as a faction separate and apart. The doctor noted that he treats about 5,000 kids – the vast majority non-Muslim – in his practice, including many low-income, vulnerable children that other doctors won't accept for insurance reimbursement reasons. His sons were born in the United States and attend schools with

American, non-Muslim classmates. One son joked with me that his non-Muslim classmates would remind him and encourage him when it was time to pray. Muslims are our neighbors, work colleagues and classmates, and believe, on the whole, in giving, contributing and neighborliness, the doctor said.

Finally, we got down to brass tacks: the fear, paranoia and hatred inspired by terrorist attacks around the world committed under the guise of Islam, and the political rhetoric leading to a deep distrust, rampant misconceptions and misguided fear among many of anything Muslim. The doctor didn't mince words. He said widespread "ignorance" is apparent. When people demonstrate "hate" toward Muslims, it is the responsibility of Muslims to "show them love and respond with compassion." I offered that his response sounded like the teaching of Martin Luther King, Jr. The doctor and his son laughed, telling me that King incorporated ideas from the Qur'an in his philosophy.

Terrorists do not express Islam the way that he and the more than 1 billion Muslims worldwide understand and practice Islam, the doctor emphasized.

The doctor acknowledged that Muslim children have suffered at times in school and other phases of life because of perceptions and generalized anger directed toward Muslims. Girls and women who wear hijabs have been especially identifiable targets.

I have to admit: I can be influenced like anyone else by messages delivered by politicians and the media and knowledge of evil acts committed under the banner of Islam, to think there is something subversive and dangerous about Muslims. I have to fight against unfounded stereotyping.

Attending the mosque's open house crystallized for me that you can't paint any religion or culture with a broad brush based upon distant, hyperbolic perceptions. Real dialog, personal observation and a seeking to learn and understand is a more rational and productive way to form judgments. Americans of all cultural, ethnic, racial and religious backgrounds would be well-served to take such an approach in this era of powder-keg emotions and reactions.

Randomness (Finding My Religion)

As a new resident of South Carolina's Charleston region, I am trying to find "community" and connect with people. That gave me the impetus to dial up religion.

I found an historic Reform Jewish congregation in Charleston to meet fellow Jews. As a by-product, perhaps I would also rediscover my religion.
So during Hanukkah, I went to my newly selected synagogue and attended the post-services social event. It was a challenge to meet people, as almost all congregants were engaged with family and friends. I loaded up on desserts and stuffed myself first – even if I didn't meet anyone with whom to connect, I'd at least leave satiated, I figured. I roamed the room without finding an unattached person. Then I positioned next to an official-looking woman with a name tag hoping to squeeze in an introduction, but she never broke from her conversation.

Finally, as the crowd began to dwindle, I randomly approached a table of four who were lingering, retirees older than me, sat down uninvited and introduced myself. I got lucky. Two of the congregants lived in Summerville, where I live, about 25 miles from the downtown Charleston congregation and likely where few other congregants live. And one of those whom I met made it her mission to welcome me to the area and serve as my de-facto tour guide and social planner. She refers to herself as a Southern Jew, having grown up in Augusta, GA.

The next day, she invited me to join her at the Summerville Farmer's Market, and for a tour of the historic downtown Summerville and the local history museum. Along the way, she introduced me to every market merchant, business owner and museum volunteer she knew.

She linked me to the loosely affiliated Jewish community in Summerville that she helps to organize and connected me with a Jewish teacher who I will soon meet. The next weekend, she invited me to join a weekly liberal political gathering at a coffee house/roastery and musical performances at a couple of funky breweries. And she is rescuing me from a lonely Christmas by inviting me to join other local Jews, Buddhists and agnostics for the traditional Chinese restaurant Christmas Day meal.

I'm not so much of a lapsed Jew as an ambivalent Jew, at least when it comes to practicing my religion as an integral component of my life. I identify with my Jewish heritage, ancestry and culture; I haven't with ritual, dogma, tradition and weekly devotion. I've interspersed my occasional efforts at integration with Jewishness with other attempts at a more faith-based life with other denominations, seeking connections, a sense of community and a deepened spirituality more than any particular religiosity.

I've done stints at a Unitarian congregation, which made sense during my interfaith marriage, and a progressive-minded non-denominational Christian congregation, largely because of its Men's Fraternity, upbeat atmosphere and focus on modern-day relevance.

But each time I drifted away, from the Jewish congregation because I felt strangely detached as a "non-observant Jew," from the Unitarian group when having young children diverted attention, and from the Christian church because I couldn't overcome my discomfort with its emphasis on Jesus.

I've circled back for another as yet fledgling venture at Judaism, my natural place in the religious world. Ironically, perhaps coming to the Deep South, where Jewish congregations are scarce compared to my previous home in the Northeast, will help me find my religion and faith community.

If that does happen, my random encounter with my new Southern Jewish friend likely will be a big reason. Even if I don't, she already has made me feel more welcome in my new community and continues to make suggestions for connections based on my interests (and even non-interests, including Carolina Shag dance classes).

Some believe nothing is random; others that everything is random. Each has merit. If nothing is random, everything has meaning. And if everything is random, it stands to reason that meaning is inherent in randomness, unless one believes that the only meaning is that there is no meaning.

Damn those philosophical brain-twisters that cause cerebral logic-center headaches! All I know is that I'll take random good fortune any time it comes my way, and my random meeting was one of those times.

Friends

It takes a conscious effort to maintain friends. It's not something I'm necessarily good at, and always something I say I want to do better. It's one of those New Year's Resolution kind of things.

You have to care for relationships, like watering a garden – friends as well as family members and intimate partners – or else they shrivel up and die, or at least lose all the energy that makes them worthwhile to maintain.

That's why in recent years I have made occasional pilgrimages to New York, from where I just returned for a weekend visit with old friends. Beforehand, I often go through the tired litany of reasons in my head debating whether I should make the trip: Am I too busy to spend the time? Do I want to spend the money on a train? Do I want to spend five hours traveling each way on a cheaper but cramped bus? What if we hit New Jersey or New York traffic? What a nightmare!

And then, I always decide to go. And I'm always glad I did.

Over a weekend, I met my roommate from college in Manhattan for lunch and a walk to his office, re-acquainting and catching up on his family and professional life. Then I spent the rest of the weekend with my roommate from my post-college sportswriter job in Florida, bumming around the city and the suburbs, scoring some free biscotti from a student he teaches whose family owns a Greenwich Village Italian restaurant. On Sunday, we convened with another old

Florida journalist roommate for another trip into the city.

It was great to see three old friends and reconnect. Spending time and surrounding ourselves with good friends, people you can confide in and care about and who support you, is one of the keys to happiness, especially as we get older and maniacal career and achievement pursuits may no longer carry the same value or satisfaction.

I'm pledging to keep in better touch with and visit friends – local and distant -- more often to keep the relationships alive and healthy. The only stumbling block is excuses that don't hold water, but I'm sure all of us make them and believe in them. It's an easy goal to say; taking action, as in most things in life, is the challenge.

A Real Memorial Day Story

I'm not proud to say that I'm like most Americans when it comes to Memorial Day. The meaning is largely lost amid the pleasures of a day off of work, backyard barbecues, the first weekend of open swimming pools, and the sense that the long days of summer are just beginning.

But I recognize that the day has deep meaning to many American families. It should be revered for the sacrifices of our military members and veterans to protect our freedoms, despite diverging opinions about our government's decisions in deploying our forces.

There was one Memorial Day that stands out for me, when I did something appropriate, traditional, meaningful and memorable. As a reporter for *The Baltimore Sun* in Carroll County, a largely rural Maryland jurisdiction, I was covering the dedication of the Carroll County Vietnam Veterans Memorial, which honored 18 county residents killed in Vietnam and one missing in action. I attended the Memorial Day military service and the dedication of the memorial that followed – three engraved panels depicting combat and humanitarian scenes and the names of the lost.

Leading up to the dedication, I interviewed and wrote features about several families who lost family members in Vietnam, and others who served in the war. Their stories were powerful and made a lasting impression on me. Those who were killed were only about 12 years older than me, barely out of high school when they enlisted and were sent to fight in a faraway land.

I was in elementary school and younger when the Vietnam War was raging, so was largely oblivious to its horrors and how it divided the nation. I have imagined what it would have been like to be these guys fighting a shadowy enemy in the jungle, not knowing whether each day could be their last.

Even 25 years after the 1990 memorial dedication, I remembered the names of one of the U.S. Army veterans I interviewed, Dennis Vonella, and Vonella's friend from Carroll County and fellow Army soldier, Joseph W. Blickenstaff Jr. (Joey Blick, as I remember Vonella called him), who died in Vietnam at age 21 in a helicopter crash. At the time of the interview, it had been 20 years since Joey Blick had died, yet I distinctly remember how palpable Vonella's memories of his buddy were and how unshakable their bond through their shared experience. As I remember, Vonella was still tight with Joey Blick's father, Joseph Blickenstaff Sr.

Out of curiosity, I looked up Dennis Vonella on the Internet, and was sad to see that he had died at the relatively young age of 58 in 2008. But what was more upsetting was the way he died, described in an article in *The Virginian-Pilot.* In retirement, Vonella had moved to a dream setting in Manteo, NC, a seaside town where he could enjoy fishing and boating, and was working as a booking agent for a cruise and fishing expedition charter service.

One night, Vonella's wife called police to their home because Dennis was despondent and threatening to commit suicide. The police report said Dennis came out of his room and fired shots at police, but none were hit and none returned fire.

Police set up a perimeter around the residence and contacted Vonella by phone. Vonella appeared on the deck and began shooting, agitated and yelling at police. He went back inside, but re-emerged and fired again. Officers returned fire, hitting and killing Vonella, who had no history of attacking police or criminal record.

The police report could not conclude whether Vonella committed "suicide by cop," but mentions it as a possibility.

Reading of Vonella's disturbing ending leads me to wonder whether he ever could have really left the dread of Vietnam behind, or come to terms with the death of his friend Joey Blick and surely others. Or whether he suffered from, and succumbed to, post-traumatic stress disorder (PTSD) that he could not resolve.

The Dennis Vonellas and Joseph Blickenstaffs of this nation are what Memorial Day really is all about -- brave men and women who sign up and ship off, with no guarantee of ever coming home. And those who may suffer in silence for the rest of their lives at what they have seen and done and experienced that the rest of us never will understand.

A Real-Life Superhero, RIP

The world lost a real-life Superhero Aug. 16, 2015.

The Caped Crusader could not defy death, like his TV counterpart did so many times when cornered by The Joker, The Riddler and Penguin, but he gave so much back to life.

Leonard B. Robinson of Owings Mills, MD was successful enough in life to indulge in creating an alter ego for himself as Batman. He obtained an authentic Batman suit, pointy Bat ears, Bat mask, Bat cape, Bat emblem, Bat belt and everything, and tricked out a custom-made black Lamborghini Batmobile that looked every bit like the one Batman and Robin drove in the 1960s TV spoof.

But he didn't turn himself into Batman just for self-indulgent kicks. He used his spot-on costume and props to visit sick children at hospitals in the Washington-Baltimore region and cheer them up, allowing them to forget about their illnesses for a while and meet a character from the big screen in the flesh.

Batman Robinson became an Internet sensation in 2012 when he was pulled over on Route 29 in Maryland by police while driving the Batmobile in costume, because of an issue with his license plates, which featured the Batman emblem. Video taken of that police stop went viral. Yet in true Batman character, Robinson's identity remained unknown publicly until a story in *The Washington Post* revealed it.

I was lucky enough to see Batman Robinson in his Batmobile once in person, on the same Route 29 where he was stopped by police. I take Route 29 to work every day. One day, while riding the bus, I saw the convertible Batmobile with Batman Robinson in full garb driving. It made my day. That guy doesn't mind standing out in the crowd, I thought. I later learned about his philanthropic mission.

Tragically, Robinson was killed on a Western Maryland highway when his Batmobile conked out, and he was struck by another car. He was 51. He will be remembered as someone who put personal eccentricity to maximum use for the public good. Just imagine the tremendous impact he had and impression he made on so many kids whose daily visitors are typically doctors, nurses and lab techs. And not only the kids, but their parents and relatives, who no doubt cried with happiness at seeing their kids' faces light up with joy.

Many of us would love to have such influence and make such an impact on others. But how many figure out how to do it like Batman Robinson did?

Batman Robinson was an original – no disrespect to Adam West. I feel privileged to have glimpsed the real deal just once. It is a fortunate man who can bring joy to so many while living out a fantasy that could give rise to the thought that, yes, maybe a regular man, like modest millionaire Bruce Wayne, really can have a "superpower" if he is creative and caring and passionate and dedicated.

Batman Robinson had a superpower. He will be sorely missed.

Swimming Toward Segregation?

I encountered something unusual at my neighborhood pool on Memorial Day: It was segregated.

That might not be unusual in America, where the norm in many places would be all-black or all-white pools, not by rule anymore, but by demographics nonetheless.

But where I live is different – at least it's supposed to be, and has been. I live in "the Next America," the name visionary developer James Rouse gave to his socially engineered and meticulously planned community between Baltimore and Washington called Columbia, MD.

Born out of the idealism and civil rights movement of the 1960s, Columbia was designed as a place where the typical practice of home builders and sellers intentionally blocking African-Americans from buying in certain developments would not be tolerated. In its early days, interracial couples purposefully moved to Columbia, recognizing its acceptance of a union that was still taboo most everywhere else.

It was consciously planned and developed as a new type of suburban city that would foster racial harmony, social integration and cultural and economic diversity. Housing types were mixed in the same community, so lawyers and laborers would live side by side.

But if my Memorial Day experience is any indication, the best-laid plans are showing cracks in their foundation.

I had just completed a class in my graduate program called "Diversity Issues in Counseling," so I have become more attuned to such issues. At 5:30 p.m. on a gorgeous, sunny holiday, it struck me after I swam my laps: I was the only white at the pool, other than the lifeguards. I made a quick count: about 35 African-Americans and one Asian family.

The area within a mile of the pool is still quite diverse – there are certainly many white residents. Could this have been an aberration, a snapshot "census count" at the pool that would rarely be replicated? Certainly. Could it be that whites are less likely to go swimming than blacks on the whole? Probably not.

Or could this be a small, inconclusive and unscientific, yet observable sign that self-segregation is occurring, in a place that was established as the national antithesis to discrimination and segregation? With 23 pools in Columbia, could white families who live closest to my neighborhood pool be consciously choosing to go to another one? Maybe.

I cannot draw a reliable conclusion from this miniscule sample, only make an observation and pose the question. However, in this same community, I have observed the trend of certain schools gaining higher proportions of minority students, as white families move to other districts.

Race is a sensitive topic in America, and open communications is an essential element to improve understanding, tolerance and connections. I don't mean to stir the pot; only to shine a light.

Ridin' Scared: Whistling Through America's Most Murderous City Park

October 16, 2015 -- Tomorrow my daughter Rebecca will run the Baltimore Marathon for the second time, quite an accomplishment for a 19-year-old. Her first marathon gave me the chance for an offbeat and slightly harebrained adventure to see her finish the race in the heart of Baltimore.

I didn't want to jam into a light rail train car at 6 a.m. or get stuck trying to maneuver and park my own car among nearly 30,000 runners and their families, so I came up with the idea to ride my bike to the start/finish area at the Orioles and Ravens stadium complex. I studied the Baltimore City map and found what looked like the most scenic and direct route to enter the city from the west, where I live.

My wife Amy and Rebecca urged me not to ride my bike all the way through Baltimore to the city center, concerned about my safety. Baltimore is notorious for being one of America's most violent cities. In 2014, the year of my bike-ride adventure on Baltimore Marathon day, the city recorded 211 murders. In the subsequent three years, Baltimore saw 344, 318 and 343 murders, respectively. But as Amy knows all too well, the more she urges me not to do something, the more determined I become to do it (Disclaimer: This particular practice is not recommended for guys as a lesson for improving your marriage.)

I drove to a Park & Ride just outside the city, embarked on my bike, and soon reached the historic

17th century mill village of Dickeyville, listed on the National Register of Historic Places, and the adjoining historic mill town of Franklintown. After riding through these pastoral, historic areas with their old stone buildings and lush greenery, I entered Leakin Park. Leakin Park was serene and beautiful, an oasis of nature in the city with streams, trails and mature forest that stretched for miles. I thought I was in the countryside.

But as soon as I emerged from Leakin Park, I entered Baltimore's West Side slums. I rode several miles through blighted streets dotted with boarded-up and vacant houses and dilapidated urban housing projects, which dominated the landscape until several blocks before the stadiums.

I had no idea about Leakin Park's reputation until more than a month later when I told my story of urban cycling to my wife's family at Thanksgiving dinner. "You rode through Leakin Park? What were you thinking!?" was their response.

It was then that I learned that Leakin Park is known as the Deadliest Park in America. It is the setting in the *Serial* true murder mystery podcast – a spinoff of *This American Life* radio show – and the site of a search for a dead body in HBO's *The Wire* about the cat-and-mouse chase between Baltimore police and drug gangs. *Serial* features the 1999 murder of high school student Hae Min Lee, whose body was found in Leakin Park. Her ex-boyfriend, Adnan Syed, was convicted and is serving a life sentence for the crime.

Leakin Park's reputation as a Dead Zone is well-deserved. It gained infamy in 1968, when four young boys were found dead in the park. Many believe that Leakin became a preferred dumping ground for bodies because of exactly what I experienced riding through it – it's on the edge of West Baltimore's crime-ridden neighborhoods, yet it feels a world away from urban blight.

Dead bodies discovered in Leakin Park have been documented as a research hobby of Ellen Worthing, who created the website Bodies of Leakin Park. Her research found that 67 bodies were discovered in Leakin Park since 1968 – a number that may actually be higher because of a six-year gap in *Baltimore Sun* library archives.

I was blissfully ignorant on my ride to the 2014 Baltimore Marathon. I was oblivious that Leakin Park was also leakin' blood, leakin' menace, leakin' secrets and leakin' revenge. I only saw one or two people during my ride through the park. Maybe I was lucky that it was 8:30 a.m. on a Saturday. Mayhem was sleeping in.

I enjoy telling the story now about my brush with death, my whistling journey through the graveyard, a 21st century Ichabod Crane on bike unwittingly fleeing the Headless Horseman. It's a nice memory and a story that is ripe for great embellishments. But you won't see me cycling through Leakin Park on Baltimore Marathon Day 2015. Body #68 will be somebody else.

What's Wrong with People and Why are Cyclists Targets of Their Stupidity?

I went for a bike ride last evening on a usual route in a semi-rural/wealthy suburban region of my county. The weather was perfect, with the sun beginning to set, and the ride was peaceful – except for the three different motorists who either hurled epithets at me or yelled and waved their arms at me from behind, apparently trying to scare me.

And all I can think is, *What the hell is wrong with these people? And why do they love making cyclists the target of their displaced anger or desire to harass or bully?* Because that's what it is.

The worst offender was the man driving in the opposite direction that I was cycling, in the opposite lane. He purposefully slowed down, pointed his arm at me out the window and yelled a few indecipherable words followed by a clear, "Faggot!" What inspires such unprovoked anger and hatred, I have no idea.

On my way back on my circuitous route, two times people yelled and screeched at me from behind and stuck arms out the window. One seemed to be a carload of teenagers. This happens often to cyclists, perpetrated by ignorant and disrespectful people who have no concept that cyclists take risks every time they ride the roads, and that being startled by a piercing scream coming from an approaching vehicle can cause a cyclist to swerve and lose balance just enough to wipe out.

I've never had the desire to yell at a cyclist from a vehicle. I don't know where that comes from. We do have a lot of anger problems in our society, and I suppose it has to get displaced somewhere. In my counseling internship, I counseled several people with nearly uncontrollable rage, including one who could be set off by a look or slightest misstep by another. They had no idea why they felt that way, but desperately wanted to get rid of it.

When I get cursed or screeched at while riding a bike, I can feel a little road rage coming on myself. I have the desire to track down the motorist and get in his face (perpetrators are always male) and yell, *What the f*** is wrong with you, a**hole!* Or at least get the license plate, though I don't know what I would do with that information. But of course the motorist is long gone before I can do anything. So I just put it in perspective, shake my head, let any feelings of anger dissolve quickly, try to feel compassion for the disturbed motorist and keep on pedaling.

Speaking of road rage, it's a growing epidemic, an indication of our frantic, largely self-absorbed society. In the last week, right in front of my son's high school, a man driving erratically during the morning commuting hours pulled out a gun and shot at another motorist, hitting the driver's side door. I can't say I would be totally surprised if someday I see a driver pointing a gun at me as I cycle the road, especially someone with explosive anger who believes I have held him up from his destination.

CHAPTER 11

Trump Nation: A Land Divided

A portion of my midlife has been marred by the cruel, corrupt, conniving and claustrophobic presidency of Donald Trump and its abject depravity, and the ascendancy of his sycophants, apologists and cultists.

I Was a Journalist, Never Equating it with Being 'Scum,' 'Low-life' and 'Disgraceful'

Donald Trump has called me a "phony," "low-life," "scum," "corrupt," "dishonest," "disgraceful," "disgusting," "illegitimate," a "horrible" person, a "terrible" person, and probably more. Those are just the insults I've heard him speak and seen in news reports. The presidential candidate's invectives are aimed at journalists – all journalists. He paints the entire profession with a broad brush, labeling it with a negative stereotype, just as he does other groups of people, like Mexican rapists and fame-hungry, lying women.

I was a journalist for 13 years after college, and hold a master's degree in journalism. Though I am not employed as a journalist now, I am still a journalist and writer at heart. My second book, a nonfiction account of my run for political office, *Don't Knock, He's Dead: A Longshot Candidate Gets Schooled in the Unseemly Underbelly of American Campaign Politics* (a timely topic given Trump's abhorrent 2016 campaign!), is journalistic in nature, combined with memoir.

I was a reporter for the *Sarasota (FL) Herald-Tribune, The Baltimore Sun,* a chain of community newspapers and several trade publications. Trump is smearing a big part of my identity with his talk about corrupt media populated by nothing but cretins. Of course, to use a favorite Trump rejoinder, he's WRONG!...WRONG!...WRONG!

At the risk of sounding about as crude as Trump, the Orange Man and some – but certainly not all – of his supporters don't know shit about journalism, what it takes to be a good journalist, what stirs the heart and soul of a journalist, and what many journalists strive for in terms of ethics, honesty, fairness and truthfulness in performing their job.

Hey Trump and your band of merry men, how about taking a break from insult-hurling and baseless fear-mongering and watch *Spotlight,* the Academy Award-winning movie about *Boston Globe* journalists who won the Pulitzer Prize following their relentless pursuit of the child sexual abuse scandal and cover-up perpetrated by the Boston-area Catholic Church leaders that extended to the top of the archdiocese and other powerful authorities? Who was the scum there? How many priests would still be shuffled along to a new church to find a new crop of boys to molest without the journalists' intervention?

And at the risk of sounding elitist, I don't expect many of Trump's supporters to understand – but merely to react to what they hear as gospel. It is common for some of Trump's supporters to take up their leader's cry at rallies and yell and point fingers at journalists and tell them, without ever having talked to them, that they are corrupt and they "suck."

Reporters and editors, on the whole, are smart, curious and highly educated. They enter journalism because they like debating ideas, considering different perspectives, thinking idealistically, learning new things, contributing to an open and just society, and educating others through expression. It would be rare for a reporter to get a job without a college degree. Fact is, the biggest cohort of Trump supporters are whites without a college education. I imagine they are some of the ones shouting down journalists as their instigator grins deviously at the podium. No clue what being a journalist truly is about.

Do journalists have biases? Yes, they all do. Everyone does. Journalists are human. Are more progressives (likely Democrats) drawn to journalism than conservatives? Probably. Are there media outlets, including newspapers, known for being conservative as well as progressive? Yes, certainly. By and large, the media outlets reflect the prevailing ideologies and sensibilities of their communities.

The *Arizona Republic,* the state's largest newspaper, had endorsed Republicans for president for the past 126 years, until breaking tradition in 2016. What happened when the newspaper broke ranks? Reporters, editors and even door-to-door subscription salespeople were greeted with screams, vitriol and even death threats.

The paper's president and publisher wrote in an emotional and defiant column: "What is the correct response, really, to this:

'YOU'RE DEAD. WATCH YOUR BACK.
WE WILL BURN YOU DOWN.
YOU SHOULD BE PUT IN FRONT OF A FIRING
SQUAD AS A TRAITOR.'
[No, not LIES! Check the primary source.]

I have known and worked with many reporters and editors. By and large, they are tough-minded, persistent, constantly digging, obsessed with facts and public records, concerned with accuracy and driven by exposing the truth and holding the feet of those in power to the fire.

I know how I acted as a journalist. And I repudiate Trump's characterization. I strived for fairness; I made the extra call, even when I knew it would be uncomfortable, in an effort to incorporate all sides and views; I was as thorough and persistent as I could be; I tried to treat all subjects I encountered with respect; I fretted about my words and their potential impact; I was ethical.

I also tried to make stories interesting and readable for an audience. Editors demanded it – good writing, flow, telling a story. This is another aspect of journalism about which Trump and his ilk have no concept. Journalists are not merely fact-reciters. I tended to fall into this trap as a journalist until good editors beat it out of me – the lazy, "He said, she said" type of story going back and forth between two sides. Instead, journalists become authorities and experts on the subjects they cover, and as they get to know their topics and sources in depth, their expertise comes through in their writing as they sift through the facts, perspectives and opinions. If a journalist knows something to be true by virtue of their reporting and facts pointing to a conclusion, it's part of their job as writers to say it with authority and back it up.

Earlier this month, the Committee to Protect Journalists issued an extraordinary warning about Trump's threat to journalists everywhere and to the U.S. Constitution's First Amendment. In part, it reads:

"Guaranteeing the free flow of information to citizens through a robust, independent press is essential to American democracy. For more than 200 years this founding principle has protected journalists in the United States and inspired those around the world, including brave journalists facing violence, censorship, and government repression.

Donald Trump, through his words and actions as a candidate for president of the United States, has consistently betrayed First Amendment values…CPJ's board of directors passed a resolution declaring Trump an unprecedented threat to the rights of journalists and to CPJ's ability to advocate for press freedom around the world."

There are plenty of reasons to recoil in disgust with Trump. His blasphemous tirade against journalists – members of one of the institutions that *truly does make America great* compared to other autocratic, oppressive nations, like Trump endlessly advertises – hits home with me more than some others.

Ink-stained wretches, nigh "scum" and "low-lifes," unite!

Democrats: 'Do the Opposite: 'Advice to Progressives in the Immediate Post-Hillary Apocalypse

A significant portion of my midlife will be lived under a Donald Trump presidency.

Given that reality, I have advice for congressional Democrats before Trump takes office: Take a page from *Seinfeld's* everyman loser George Costanza playbook, and "Do the Opposite."

Democrats understandably will feel compelled to fight Trump and the Republican ruling class, and even though they don't have the numbers, attempt to obstruct, as the GOP strategically did to Obama. Don't do it. Resist the urge. Be compliant. Be like rubber. Learn from these insightful, introspective reflections from George Costanza:

"It's just not working."

"Every instinct I have…it's all been wrong."

"Bald men with no jobs and no money who live with their parents don't approach strange women."

Democrats are now the bald men with no jobs and no money who live with their parents. So let the Republicans have their day…or four years. They're expecting you to fight, posture, contest, provoke, make noise, level charges, hurl criticism, erect barriers, whine and complain. Don't. Do the opposite.

Sure, try to do some nibbling around the edges of the Republican agenda, budget and bills, where maybe they'll accept a stray amendment to shut you up. But otherwise, be the matador, and let the bull charge through your cape.

Let the Republican agenda unfold, whole and unfettered and unadulterated and without significant compromise. It's the only way America will discover whether the GOP is imbued with brilliance or folly, whether Republicans have been blowhards full of hot air and empty rhetoric or they're really onto something prescient, whether they're firmly grounded or living in an alternate reality, whether they distinguish fact from fiction.

We have a baseline and trend lines to start with. Memorialize those. Let the GOP agenda play out over four years. Ensure nonpartisan experts analyze and document the results and make projections on future course. Four years should be enough time to indicate clear trends, if not definitive outcomes.

Only then will we know more conclusively whether the nation has suffered or gained, and who has done the suffering or gaining. Will people be hurt in the process? Possibly, but it will be the only way to know. If the Republican Emperor is shown to have no clothes, he will be naked with nowhere to hide in the 2018 and 2020 elections.

What will have happened to health care costs, health care accessibility and the ranks of the uninsured?

Will millions of manufacturing jobs have been created, or "brought back?"

What will the economic indicators show?

What will be America's status in global trade and what will it mean to industry and the economy?

Will America be viewed internationally as a treasured ally or as an isolationist with a case of the heebie-jeebies?

Will ISIS still be living strong or dead?

What will have happened to families that include an illegal immigrant?

Will there be a Mexico-U.S. wall, and if so, at what cost and benefit?

Will America be more united or more divided?

Will the swamp be draining or flooding?

Will those screaming for change be better or worse off?

Will Americans perceive the country on the "right" or "wrong" track.

Will the environment be renewed or denuded?

Will America be relying more heavily again on coal or "clean energy," and what will be the effects of either path?

Will inner cities be revived? How will African-Americans in those areas answer Trump's question: "What have you got to lose?"

We can then examine the evidence and facts (if indeed, either still have any currency), and know with a high degree of certainty where credit or blame lies. Then America will have a chance to make another judgment in a more transparent, less muddled environment on Trump and the GOP's ideas and execution, out in the open, naked, with nowhere to hide and no Obama or Hillary to scapegoat.

It worked for George Costanza. It was unpredictable, confounding, paradoxically brilliant. Doing the same thing never worked for George. But doing the opposite...Anything could happen.

A Nation Consumed by Anger

November 5, 2016 -- Mercifully, the 2016 U.S. presidential election campaign is nearly over. (Or at least, we can hope. God only knows what Nov. 9, 2016 will bring.) And through all the shenanigans, rhetoric, nonsense, hyperbole, deflection, rationalization, hot air and blasphemy, I'm left with one overriding impression: the raw anger and mean-spiritedness of so many Americans. It's pervasive and seemingly contagious. And quite disturbing and unsettling. I'm predicting we'll see the intensity increase after the results are in.

One of my counseling texts describes unconstrained anger as "a tendency to hold something or someone else responsible." When an individual holds something or someone external responsible for their stress, anxiety, or frustration, they often feel they "have the right to express it in an aggressive manner."

The nation is afflicted with this malady of "blaming the other" now: It's the Mexicans taking jobs and committing crimes; it's trade agreements shipping jobs away; it's the Syrian refugees; it's the Muslims; it's all immigrants; it's the nefarious, corrupt Clintons; it's the socialists and liberals; it's the Religious Right and evangelicals; it's all of Washington; it's the politicians; it's Obamacare; it's the media; it's the police; it's racism; it's sexism; it's greed; it's Wall Street; it's Big Business; it's the liars, cheaters and fraudsters.

Topping the list of managing anger, says the text, is acknowledging this: "You are responsible for your own life, the choices you make, and the quality of your life experience."

I would argue that too many Americans have been sold a bill of goods called "The American Dream." While such a highfalutin concept certainly exists -- America offers ample opportunity to achieve some self-defined measure of success -- it is not a guarantee for everyone. Hard work doesn't guarantee it. So many other variables are at play outside an individual's control. And the illusory American Dream also should not be confused with happiness. The Declaration of Independence grants Americans "the pursuit of happiness" but not happiness. That must be arrived at internally, through mind, body, soul and spirit.

I expect too many Americans expect or want something that they do not have, or thought their lives would be different -- better, more successful, without constant struggle, disappointment and limitations (self-imposed or otherwise). Too many Americans abdicate taking responsibility for their own lives, the quality of their lives, and their choices. They are not happy with who they are, where they are, what they have chosen, what they do, the people around them or the quality of their daily existence. It is difficult to change. It takes personal responsibility and risk to change. And it would be too painful to blame themselves. The anger has to be released somewhere, so individuals displace it toward convenient targets, and sometimes, literally, to anyone who crosses their path. Why else road rage? Why else scream down a reporter one has never met?

Yes, this is a bit of pop psychology. It's based on no research, no surveys. It's anecdotal. Yet there is no doubt that anger in America is palpable, visceral, barely contained and exploding in spots. Post-election has powder keg written all over it. And I can't help but think that to find the true source and cause of this anger, Americans have to stop looking outward and take a hard look at themselves.

No More 'Working for The Man' Just for Health Insurance

On the eve of the first Obamacare (Affordable Care Act) mano-a-mano showdown in Congress in 2017 – well, at least the participants were in the same boxing ring – I re-emphasize my position that after all the overinflated chatter is aired and convoluted schemes are floated, the only real, efficient, cost-effective and sustainable solution is a single-payer health care system (Medicare for All, universal health care coverage).

I'll give the Republicans a chance, with their Repeal and Replace initiative (or Repeal and Posture, or Repeal and Delay, or Repeal and High-Five) and monitor the trends and see where we are a few years after implementation. Democrats should not participate in crafting an Obamacare Replacement, so it will be a pristinely GOP invention without Democratic fingerprints and can be evaluated as such.

Obamacare certainly has had positive impacts. A December 2016 Commonwealth Fund report found the percentage of uninsured working age adults declined in every state by 2015, as did uninsured rates for low-income adults.

Why write about Obamacare as a midlife issue? Because I'm one step away from needing health insurance through a system like Obamacare, and I may need that program or something similar in the future as I grapple with transition and living authentically in midlife. In my transition to a new career as a mental health counselor, I eventually had to leave full-time employment to meet my graduate program's internship and class requirements. And with that move went my health insurance. I was lucky I have a wife with an employer-sponsored plan that I could join. But we all know how tenuous are jobs – and the potluck health insurance that may come with them – in today's economy.

I've written about joining the Gig Economy since my transition, working multiple part-time, temporary, or entrepreneurial jobs with no health insurance or other benefits to cobble together an income. While I may sometime again have a full-time job with health insurance benefits, I plan to stay a member of the Gig Economy for the rest of my career by establishing an independent counseling practice. And I abhor the thought of health insurance posing a major barrier to venturing out on my own and pursuing my dream.

A single-payer health care system, or perhaps an Obamacare-like system, could remove that impediment for me and many others with an entrepreneurial bent who no longer want to be obligated to 'working for The Man' just so they can have health insurance.

I wrote extensively about the merits of a nonprofit single-payer system and the advantages and pitfalls of Obamacare in my political memoir about my campaign for Maryland delegate, *Don't Knock, He's Dead: A Longshot Candidate Get Schooled in the Unseemly Underbelly of American Campaign Politics,* as advocating for a more equitable, less costly health care system was a cornerstone of my campaign.

No Democratic Lifeline for 'Repeal and Replace'

Senate minority leader Chuck Schumer said if congressional Republicans, in conjunction with President-elect Donald Trump's exhortations, vote to repeal Obamacare, Democrats won't participate in crafting a so-called "replacement."

"If they repeal without a replacement, they will own it," Schumer told *The Washington Post.* "Democrats will not then step up to the plate and come up with a half-baked solution that we will partially own. It's all theirs."

I agree wholeheartedly with Schumer's approach and urge Democrats to stick to that plan, instead of capitulating to the Republicans and trying to modify or soften whatever plan the GOP hatches once health care coverage is thrown into uncertainty, or worse, chaos, and millions potentially suffer.

To do so would be akin to the Democrats turning over ownership of a marginally inhabitable building to the Republicans, who level it with a wrecking ball and wander aimlessly through the rubble, only to have the Democrats return with hard hats and shovels and mortar to salvage the wreckage, with the promise, "We'll help you rebuild from these ruins, but we gotta warn ya, dollars to donuts, this building will be condemned."

As I advised Democrats previously, Do The Opposite, like Seinfeld's George Costanza. The GOP will expect Democrats to come running to save the day for people who may be losers in the Obamacare tug-of-war. Then they will become complicit in whatever is enacted. Then they can be blamed for screwing up whatever plan

Republicans wanted to enact in the first place, which of course will be the reason said GOP plan isn't working as effectively as touted. Don't do it. Let the GOP plan ride; measure the results.

I argued in my political memoir detailing my campaign for Maryland state political office, *Don't Knock, He's Dead: A Longshot Candidate Gets Schooled in the Unseemly Underbelly of American Campaign Politics*, that Obamacare is largely a piece of legislative manure that leaves the foxes – the health insurance industry – guarding the henhouse, but that it's certainly an improvement and does a number of good things for people who need health insurance.

"Obamacare is a Rubik's Cube—lots of turning, spinning, head-scratching, reverses, glitches, bad moves and confusion," I wrote in Don't Knock, He's Dead. "Historic and groundbreaking yet torturously overwrought, the law certainly does some good, but adds yet another layer of preposterous bureaucracy and complexity and supposed 'consumer choice,' which really is massive consumer overload and confusion, onto a preexisting byzantine miscreation, and will become another cement-hardened convention impossible to undo."

My campaign for Maryland state delegate in 2014 was largely based on advocating for accessible, affordable health care for all – universal health care, single-payer health care, Medicare for All – whatever you want to label it. My call was for a system that covered *everyone*, regardless of employment status or personal wealth, one that constituted a right rather than a privilege, and that reduced the corporate profit motive. It was for a more humane system that would put Maryland – and ideally, ultimately, the rest of the nation – in line with the rest of the democratic, industrialized nations that provide all their citizens basic health care at about half the cost or less per person than the U.S., and achieve better health outcomes on many common measures.

Numerous grassroots and health care organizations continue advocating for such a system, and several state legislatures have made attempts to establish one. But entrenched, opposing, big-money interests are strong – hence, Obamacare was the best we could get.

Wendell Potter, a health insurance public relations executive turned industry critic, nailed the dynamic in his insider tell-all book *Deadly Spin,* as I quoted in *Don't Knock, He's Dead.*

"The health insurance industry is dominated by a cartel of large, for-profit corporations…[T]he top priority…is to 'enhance shareholder value.' When that's your top priority, you are motivated more by the obligation to meet Wall Street's relentless profit expectations than by the obligation to meet the medical needs of your policyholders."

I still believe a single-payer system is the only real, equitable, sustainable solution to the ongoing health care mess. Perhaps a failed "replacement plan" full of tired old ideas like Medical Savings Accounts and insurance sold across state lines and free market competition that can be laid squarely at the feet of Republicans could stoke a revival of a single-payer revolution.

Of course, that will bring out the critics and naysayers who will charge that single-payer is an un-American, "socialist" system, an asinine argument. What is Medicare? What is Medicaid? What is Social Security? Socialistic! For that matter, what are our police forces and fire departments and transportation systems and public schools and state universities? Socialistic! We all contribute toward them because these systems and institutions are deemed to be beneficial to society collectively. American rugged individualism is a great concept. But in some aspects, like outstanding health care and the overall health of our citizenry, we are all in this together, and will be stronger as a nation for that.

So, as Schumer said, no lifeline. There could be regression and pain in the short-term, but maybe it could turn the tide for the long-term.

CHAPTER 12

Death

Solidarity Amid Tragedy: A Ride for Tom

I spent New Year's Day 2015 attending a funeral of sorts for someone I had never met. It was a moving event, literally and figuratively. Maybe 1,000 or more avid cyclists and casual riders alike gathered in Baltimore at the Episcopal Cathedral of the Incarnation – a starting point with sad significance -- and took over the streets in a sea of bikes on a 35 degree day as the sun faded, riding in solidarity to the spot where a cyclist was killed by a drunk and distracted driver.

Tom Palermo, a cyclist, bike frame maker, professional, married father of two young children died Dec. 27, 2014 when hit from behind while riding in a bike lane on one of Baltimore's more bike-friendly streets. The crime has attracted national and even international attention because of its egregious nature and the status of its perpetrator. Tom was run down by the second highest ranking bishop in Maryland's Episcopal Church hierarchy, who had a flagrant previous arrest for driving under the influence. This time, the bishop drove away from the accident scene with a shattered windshield with a big hole in it from where Tom crashed through it. She returned to the scene later only after cruising by and being noticed by another cyclist who stopped to render aid, and who chased her down. She has been charged with manslaughter, driving with a .22 blood alcohol level (legal limit .08), texting while driving and leaving the scene of an accident.

When I heard news of the accident and the impromptu plan for a New Year's Day memorial ride for Tom, I felt compelled to be there. If there was ever a case where the saying, "There but for the grace of God go I" applied, it was this one. I imagine all the cyclists felt the same kinship. I had spent half of 2014 campaigning for Maryland state delegate, and used my bike as a campaign tool to go door to door and to advertise. The bike was equipped with a trailer with campaign signs on each side and in back. It did not earn enough votes to win, but it made campaigning more enjoyable and kept me in shape.

However, I was often keenly aware how vulnerable I was – much more so than the one- to three-week long bike trips I've taken in my younger days. Most of the roads I traveled had no bike lanes or even shoulders, and traffic that could hit 40-50 mph or more. Drivers often seemed in a rush and distracted, oblivious to me. I was always one driver mistake away from meeting the same fate as Tom.

The Baltimore cyclists rode three or four miles on Jan. 1 to a makeshift memorial with flowers and candles and messages where the accident happened, and solemnly observed a memorial session with Tom's family and bicycle advocates as a community. A white "ghost bike" was locked to a pole in Tom's memory. Many were angry – a homemade memorial featuring a bike wheel and bike seat stood in the road's median, with the seat inscribed with "I Am Angry." But this was a time to remember Tom and support his family. Justice would have to be sought later.

The vast majority of the people at the ride had never met Tom, just like me. But there was an unmistakable feeling of connection, of familiarity. Tom was us, Tom was me. He was 10 years younger than me, but in ways similar. He had a boy and a girl, just like me, two years apart, just like me. He loved to ride, just like me. At his memorial, his family talked about how hard it was for Tom to find time to ride in recent times, with a young family, a full time job as a software engineer at Johns Hopkins Hospital and a side business. I could relate to that; when my kids were 6 and 4, free time was at a premium.

On a sunny and relatively mild December Saturday afternoon, Tom had been able to carve out some time for himself and had gone out for a ride, and never came back. It was unbelievably, crushingly, maddeningly sad.

The light amid the darkness was the spontaneous reaction of people to be there, that people cared about what happened and showed it through their actions in what can often be a cold and uncaring world. That it mattered to be there. That all the texting and Twittering and Facebooking could not substitute for being present, for joining a brotherhood and sisterhood with a common avocation to acknowledge one of their own. I had debated whether or not to go – it was cold, I wanted to relax at home on a day off. But when the time came, I knew I would regret inaction, so I went and I'm glad I did. It was among the most moving events I have ever experienced, largely because of its spontaneity. A thousand cyclists claiming their piece of ownership of the streets – if only for an hour – is quite a spectacular sight.

As I have reached well into midlife, I have become more and more aware of mortality. This is nothing unusual. But incidents like Tom's just serve to remind me – I don't know when my number is up. Life does feel more precious; it becomes more urgent to strive for fulfillment, meaning and self-actualization. Perhaps there does come a point in everyone's life when there is no more time to wait for tomorrow or someday. A week or so after Tom's accident, we heard about ESPN's Stuart Scott – BOOYAH! – passing away after a long fight with cancer. He was two years younger than me.

I imagine I will often think of Tom when I ride. I have thought about him every day since the memorial ride. And like every other cyclist there that day – I would bet my life on this – I am not going to stop riding the roads. It comes with some risk, but so does life.
I never knew Tom, but I wish I did. I have a feeling I would have liked him. I wish the best for his family.

Facing a Match Point

It has not really been intentional, but death has been a recurring theme in my essays about midlife. There was cyclist Tom Palermo, tragically mowed down in the prime of life by a drunk bishop. Two co-workers at my current job have been at work one day, gone the next. Perhaps it's inevitable that when you reach midlife, feelings of immortality are stripped and death becomes less an abstract concept and more a certainty you have to reckon with. And that can be a good thing, motivation to be your real self, focus on the things that are most important and for which you have the most passion, take more risks, express yourself more fully and love more deeply.

This essay, however, is about life, not death, though its specter, I would imagine, is present, a hard thing to dance around. It is about the fight for life and the preciousness of life. It is about braving the worst of times so one day again the best of times will feel even sweeter. It is about having to dive deeper into one's soul and mine further into one's spirit than ever previously imagined. It is about adjusting and learning new ways of living, being and relating.

I received an e-mail from my tennis buddies that a friend – really an acquaintance, but I know if I knew him better, he would be a friend – had been diagnosed with colon cancer. Bobby, who has two kids, is a tennis pro at the clubs where I play, and has coached at the high school and college levels. We have crossed paths and talked a number of times. I know something about his job from personal experience.

After a layoff from a public relations job in 2002, I got certified as a tennis instructor from the U.S. Professional Tennis Registry. I had been a competitive junior and college tennis player, and had always been interested in teaching – especially competitive juniors – but never had the time. Now I did. I taught for a while for the same recreational organization where Bobby teaches, spent a summer teaching at a summer camp, and coached a girls high school team. I made an arrangement with a local swim and tennis club to teach members and non-members on its two seldom-used courts, and began building up a clientele. I taught for a nonprofit organization that ran after-school programs, and eventually became its organizer and director of a high school training program. I loved it, but as I eventually re-entered the corporate world, my tennis teaching started to dwindle. At one point, I talked to Bobby about assisting him with his juniors program, but it never came to pass.

I only describe my own experience with tennis teaching because I know that as a successful tennis teacher and coach, Bobby possesses many attributes that are going to help him in his fight to recover. Any successful tennis coach must have energy, passion, enthusiasm, patience, positivity and spirit. That's what rubs off on students and keeps adults and kids coming back and hooked on working to improve their games. I can tell Bobby possesses these traits by his community's outpouring of love and support. He has had an impact, likely far broader than he ever thought. As an individual sport, tennis teaches many life lessons: managing emotions; staying positive; focusing on the moment; having a game plan, and adjusting when it's not working; dealing with adversity; valuing the process as much or more than the results; and fighting hard and never giving up. These, too, can be applied to Bobby's challenge.

Bobby is somewhere in his 40s, younger than I am and too young for this. For me, as with the story of cyclist Tom Palermo's death on a weekend ride, this hits home as another case of "there but for the grace of God go I." Life is unfair. And for Bobby, this sucks. But I notice he is already learning new things.

When I e-mailed him about writing about his journey, he responded that he had learned from the outpouring of community support to "put my pride and privacy to the side and allow people that want to help to do so." We all have our walls and our desire to be invulnerable. In acknowledging vulnerability, I believe Bobby is letting some walls down. And in so doing, he will be letting in the caring and love that will strengthen him to beat his illness. I'm praying for him and his family, and hope with all my heart I see him out on the court with his students, hitting balls and barking encouragement, come spring and summer.

The Intersection of Beginning and Ending

For the second straight day, I couldn't get my mother on the phone and got no reply to my messages. The last time I called from work and left a message, I got a sick feeling. I knew something was wrong.

I called my wife Amy and told her to meet me at my mother's apartment building, where we had struggled to move her a year earlier during a period of my mother's physical health decline and struggle with a mental health disorder. At midlife, roles had reversed and we had become my mother's caretakers and support system.

When we got no response to our knock on the door, dread came over me. We entered and found her dead on the bathroom floor, cause of death unknown. Though she had been experiencing health problems, they were more the nagging kind than life-threatening—until they were even more than that, suddenly.

It was a tragic start to a political campaign. Only five days earlier, I had registered in Maryland's capital of Annapolis as a Democratic candidate for state delegate. I had never told my mother I was considering running—our relationship had been strained during her time of unpredictable and volatile mental health, exacerbated by her stubborn nature and rebellious streak. I didn't want to mention a political run until I was fully committed to entering the race and felt she was on firmer ground. I had planned to let her know I was in the race the next time I saw her. I never got that opportunity. I felt terrible I had never shared the news.

The profile story on my candidacy in the *Baltimore Sun* with an October 8, 2013 dateline coincidentally hit the newsstands the same day that Amy and I found my mother dead. That day, I was going to proudly present the article to my mother, my biggest supporter, as I broke the news to her about my candidacy.

I wrote about my mother's political influence on me and the impact of her death on my nascent campaign in *Don't Knock, He's Dead: A Longshot Candidate Gets Schooled in the Unseemly Underbelly of American Campaign Politics:*

I credit my mother Sandra Sachs, a diehard liberal Democrat from Boston who had a fascination with the Massachusetts Kennedy clan, a devotion to other charismatic pols and a penchant for volunteering for campaigns, for getting me interested in politics...

The Sun article provided me a nice opening salvo. Now I just had to back it up with real action. That is, as soon as I could plan a memorial service for my mother, meet and make plans with funeral directors, coordinate with out-of-town family, untangle her financial affairs, launch the bureaucratic estate settlement process with the Register of Wills, negotiate with her landlord, make repairs to her apartment, sell her furniture on Craigslist, and move all her other belongings out of her apartment within three weeks. Not the ideal way or frame of mind to launch a campaign.

So the first month of my campaign was put virtually on hold while I dealt with my mother's affairs and coped with the sudden loss emotionally. In a spiritual way, I felt Sandra Sachs with me during the campaign, watching over me as I traveled door-to-door and marched with people who were struggling day-to-day. It occurred to me that maybe it was fate that I was running at all. It was my mother who loved politics and took pride in identifying herself as a Democrat, the party of inclusion and champion of the vulnerable, with her roots as the daughter of Eastern European immigrants who settled in the gritty outskirts of Boston and who lived a hardscrabble, working-class life. She would have been proud, I thought, looking down. No one from my family had ever run for political office before. The Kennedys we were not.

My mother's keen interest in politics landed her on Capitol Hill as a staffer for U.S. Senators Bill Bradley (D-NJ), who ran for president in 2000, and Daniel Moynihan (D-NY), no small feat for a woman who spent her initial post-college years in the 1960s into the 1970s raising kids, and then battled back from debilitating depression to gain a foothold in the workforce.

At one candidates' forum in particular, at a large residential retirement community outside of Baltimore, I felt my mother's presence with me. I eschewed my usual stump speech in favor of an effort to connect with the seniors on an emotional and personal level, as excerpted from *Don't Knock, He's Dead:*

"I have a good idea of the issues you have faced and your current challenges," I told the Charlestown [Retirement Community] residents, "but not because I read it or heard a policy wonk or a politician talk about them. I know from personal experience, from trying to help my mother with problems the last couple of years of her life before she died, when her health was going downhill."

I told them about my mother's challenges with downsizing and finding appropriate housing; exploring assisted living facilities; searching for viable transportation when she couldn't drive; navigating a poorly coordinated, frustrating health care system; determining finances; and finding social outlets. I wasn't aiming for sympathy, but nevertheless several of the attendees and my fellow candidates offered me condolences and said my speech was heartfelt afterwards. Once again, I didn't know if my speech had earned me any votes, but I was proud that it was memorable.

Nearly four years later, following a dinner celebrating my daughter Rebecca's graduation May 20, 2017 from the University of Maryland, Rebecca told me she was sad that Nana – my mother – wasn't there to celebrate with us. Another prideful campaign sadly missed. Whenever Maryland plays the University of Michigan, often now that Maryland is in Michigan's athletic conference, Rebecca said she'll think of her grandmother, who took great pride in transcending her poor, neurotic family in working class Malden,

Massachusetts to arrive at a beacon of rah-rah American collegiate life in Ann Arbor, Michigan, and who ingrained the "Go Blue!" Michigan chant in her grandkids.

And I'll always think of my mother when I recall my run for politics, one of her other great loves.

Use Your Time Wisely

Death is an unpleasant topic. Naturally, people want to avoid thinking about it. I'm no different. Whenever my wife, the ultimate planner, wants to talk to me about making plans and arrangements for my own inevitable death, like an advance health directive, so she and our kids aren't clueless about my wishes or forced to shell out money for services I neglectfully avoided covering, I balk or change the subject.
But when you reach midlife, inevitably you start confronting the reality of mortality more frequently. In 2016, that reality has hit me harder.

During one two-week stretch, two vital fathers in their 40s who were involved professionally in the tennis industry – one instructor whom I knew and the other a friend of a tennis academy owner for whom I was working – each died. The teacher I knew, Bobby Hoffman, was stricken with cancer. The other died unexpectedly of a heart attack.

Recently, my father's partner's daughter, in her early 50s, who I got to know well during several visits, was found dead of unknown causes. A few weeks later, my father's partner also passed away suddenly, with grief perhaps a contributing factor.

Earlier in the year, I discovered a woman I had dated when we were both in our 20s, who went on to achieve remarkable success in the newspaper business, had died of breast cancer at 49.

I only have one surviving parent, and he's closing in on 80. His brother, my beloved uncle, died in 2000 of juvenile diabetes shy of 60.

This essay feels like a real downer as I write it. But as a counselor-in-training who embraces the existential theory of counseling – the search for meaning and purpose and concepts such as free will and individual responsibility to chart our destiny – death is an inescapable aspect of life that, if acknowledged and confronted, can be used by individuals to maximize their potential, deepen relationships, set and pursue goals, determine priorities and enhance the joy of living.

There comes a point in life where we are hit like a brick between the eyes to tell us we don't have forever, like it once seemed. It sounds trite, but it's true and a lesson learned only with maturity: It's what we do with the time we do have that gives life its meaning. Time is our most precious commodity. It's cliché, but true again: We don't know how much time we have. Bobby Hoffman didn't; my tennis buddy's friend certainly didn't. And the greatest shame would be to piss it away.

CHAPTER 13

Weekend Warrior: Physical Fitness, Injury, and Staving off Aging

Down and Out

Lying on my back, looking up at the stars and stadium lights and the sweaty faces circling me, the terrifying thought flashed through my mind: "I'll never be the same again."

Seconds before, a crossing pass came rolling slowly from the sideline toward our goalie box. As a defender, I instinctively broke for the ball. I also broke my self-preservation rule – avoid reckless collisions – but I couldn't predict it soon enough. As I got to the ball, so did a strapping young opponent, coming full-speed. He swung his leg like a nine-iron, attempting to score. Players arriving for the next game said they heard the "thwwaaackk" a field away. I went down. I thought it might be bad, but didn't know. Just a bad bruise? I was afraid to look.

Play stopped. Players gathered around me. "Probably a broken shin guard," I heard. Someone helped take off my shin guard. It was fine. I peered haltingly at my lower right leg and knew I wasn't. We had a surgeon on the team. All she could offer was, "I'm sorry, Adam."

Another teammate gripped my hand. Others began asking me questions. "What's your wife's number?" "Which car is yours?" "Where's your bag?" Within minutes, I was being wheeled by paramedics to an ambulance. "What's your birthday?" they asked, the first of many times I would hear that question that night, to evaluate my alertness, I guess. That and, "What's your pain level, 1 to 10?"

I stayed conscious and alert through the trip to the ER, surprising myself that I didn't go into shock or even feel overwhelmed by pain. I had a broken tibia and fibula, two main bones of the leg – a "tib-fib" in orthopedic jargon. The next day I had surgery, a rod and screws inserted, and embarked on the greatest test of adversity in my life.

I had made it to 49 without ever being seriously injured or having surgery. In an instant, to go from sprinting to (pardon the political incorrectness) crippled, is an absolute shock. Prognosis: full recovery, 6 to 9 months. I would learn in the coming months that the injury and surgery didn't just affect an isolated part of my leg, but distressed my toes, foot, ankle, Achilles, calf muscle, knee – the whole kinetic chain.

I had played in a high-caliber co-ed recreational soccer league for seven years, starting at age 42 – 30 years after last playing. I stuck with it long enough to become a decent defender, and eventually team captain when no one else wanted the job.

More than 125 games, with nothing more than the occasional pulled muscle or bruised rib. It became a point of pride to be perhaps the oldest player in the league, competing against former high school and college players in their 20s and 30s, but it was getting harder.

Maybe I Should Have Quit

Maybe ego got in the way, or nostalgia, trying to recapture a vestige of youth. Maybe I should have quit. I almost did several times, but decided "just one more season." Now, barely able to bend my knee or get off the couch without great pain, I punished myself mercilessly for that decision.

I was angry at the player who hurt me. Problem was, I had no idea who he was. I was told he stood behind me as I lied on the turf that night, looking concerned. But I never heard from him. With no external target, I turned my anger and blame inward. I blamed myself for decisions I made from two seconds before the accident to months beforehand that could have changed the devastating outcome:

"I shouldn't have gone for that 50-50 ball."

"Why did I go back in the game as a sub in the second half?"

"If I had only registered for a Thursday night graduate school course instead of Wednesday, I would have missed the season."

In the first month after my injury, I continually ruminated about these scenarios, often in the wee hours of the morning between restless bouts of sleep and groggy interludes of cable TV movies and cheesy mystery novels – but of course it changed nothing.

With a walker, just like the near-death seniors at the assisted living facility up our street, I struggled to make it to the end of our 50-yard row of townhouses, and needed my wife to bring a chair so I could rest for the trip back home. Going upstairs on my butt was a chore, so the living room became my bedroom. I didn't take a real shower for weeks.

Interminable Days, Sleepless Nights

I missed three weeks of work, which was just as well because I couldn't focus, and didn't drive or wear a shoe for two months. Cooped up and growing depressed, the days became interminable, and I dreaded trying to sleep at night. I had in-home physical therapy – boring and sometimes painful leg exercises, with a lady who scolded me that I would have trouble growing old with my downbeat attitude. But I did the exercises religiously, structured my day around them, multiple sets per day, even strapping a dumbbell or a big flashlight to my heavy, protective knee-high boot to strengthen my leg. But it atrophied anyway.
I was miserable and wallowing in self-pity. If I kept it up, I wouldn't have blamed my wife if she had walked out, "in sickness" be damned.

I had been athletic all my life -- a collegiate tennis player who still played competitively – and now I was struggling to do a lap around our kitchen and living room on crutches without falling. I had the distinct feeling that the world was going on without me.

I started outpatient physical therapy with great trepidation. I imagined the therapists as heartless drill sergeants, pushing me to do masochistic exercises to see how much pain I could endure before collapsing in humiliation. Wrong. I soon embraced my sessions as part of my recovery.

In my early days of rehab, my favorite part of the day was just before bed, after a hot shower, when I lied on the bed and strapped an ultrasound bone-healing unit to my leg for 20 minutes and watched the NBA playoffs, forgetting about everything. I found myself empathizing deeply with players who suffered leg injuries – Derrick Rose of the Chicago Bulls and Baron Davis of the New York Knicks – *now really knowing* what an arduous road they faced.

Turning a Corner

I turned the corner and began rejoining life when I learned to use crutches more confidently. I would break up a work-from-home day with a laborious 1/5-mile walk to the neighborhood park about the speed of a kindergartner on 90-degree June days, sweating through my shirt and exhausting my arms, collapsing on the bench for a Gatorade break before the return trip. At night, I would take one of my kids with me until sunset.

I got stronger. I began going distances, about a mile along a path to the Lakefront in town for summer festivals and concerts, and just to sit on a bench with my son.

In late June, two months in, I mustered the courage to go to the neighborhood pool for laps. For the rest of the summer, I swam like my life depended on it, rarely missing a day, often closing down the pool after work. As the pools closed for the summer and healing progressed, I transitioned to cycling and gradually added tennis to the regimen in late fall, slowly increasing my lateral movement.

My new physical therapist told me recovery would be like a rollercoaster, and it has been. I went from two crutches, to one crutch, to no crutches, then back to one crutch as pain in my knee and swelling in my ankle made my gait uneven, then again to two crutches for a while, before finally weaning my way off. Pain and discomfort has flared and subsided regularly. But like the surgeon said, in my eighth month, I started feeling closer to normal, like this too shall pass.

Throughout my ordeal, I progressed from denial to acceptance to ownership. Ironically, the graduate course I was taking at the time of the injury was Theological Anthropology – an exploration of the influence and meaning of God and spirituality in our lives and the world. I came to view my injury as having deeper meaning – the response to adversity, nobility in suffering, a preparation for things to come. I didn't even want to trade it away anymore, because then it wouldn't even be *my life*, my unique experience, but someone else's.

It was tremendously humbling. Who are you if you can't do what you've always done? It gave me the perspective of living with a disability. I parked in "handicapped" spaces. Near-strangers asked what happened and offered their sympathy, welcomed or not. With my crutches and boot, I felt like a conversation piece.

It ate away at me that the player who injured me had never contacted me. I guess I just wanted to think it mattered...I mattered. Just after Thanksgiving, seven months after the injury, I e-mailed the player's captain to say I was recovering and that I forgave his teammate. He responded that his teammate felt really bad about it, and it was his idea to send me the Get Well card with a $50 Amazon gift card way back when.

I still never heard directly from that player, and never will. But I never thought about it again. I guess that's part of learning how to heal – physically, mentally, and spiritually.

Thanks Dr. Dave

April 26, 2016 -- Four years ago April 26, I suffered one of the worst nights of my life. One moment I was playing rec league soccer, running after a 50-50 ball. The next, after a reverberating THUD, I was on my back, dazed, wondering what had just happened. It only took a second to realize I had a shattered leg, and within minutes, paramedics were hoisting me onto a transportable bed and loading me into an ambulance.

On the ride to the hospital, I realized my life had suddenly changed. My immediate fear was that I would never be the same again. I had never been injured that badly before.

With the knowledge gleaned from my counseling classes and experience in counseling clients in my current internship, I would hope I would be able to think more positive and optimistic thoughts in the future when something bad happens to me. I struggled to overcome negative thinking and emotions in the early stages of my recovery. I was told I would have a full recovery, but I couldn't help having doubts.

I often pass the field where I was injured, on the way to and from my university, including at night, when the field lights are bright, just as I remember from my back while staring into the dark sky on the night I got hurt. It brings back memories that I now embrace as an experience integral to my life. It wasn't cancer, I wasn't dying, and I'm grateful for that, but it was a type of adversity I had never faced before.

At this time of year, I also always remember the doctor who performed the surgery to put my leg back together. In an amazing coincidence, it turned out the surgeon lived in my same townhome community, but I did not know him. In a sign that I'm getting older, Dr. Dave was about 15 years my junior. After the surgery, as I was hobbling around the neighborhood on crutches, I would run into Dr. Dave walking his dog. He would always challenge me to do a little more than I thought I was capable of – put more weight on my leg, begin walking sooner. We became friendly.

Dr. Dave eventually moved to California to specialize in spinal surgery. It took more than a year to recover to 90 percent or more. But just more than a year after surgery, I completed a triathlon. A neighbor who was at the event texted Dr. Dave, who replied, "Awesome!"

I did the triathlon again two years later, three years after surgery. That time I got Dr. Dave's number and texted him myself to let him know how grateful I was for his skill and expertise, and that I was as close to 100 percent as I could be. Dr. Dave was glad to hear it, but to him, it was probably no big deal. That's just what he does, he fixes broken people. Still, I figure doctors who heal probably don't always hear the appreciation and gratefulness for their work after the patient disappears.

I will be forever grateful for Dr. Dave. He gave me my life back – at least the physical life that I knew and only fully appreciated after it was taken away. I will honor Dr. Dave with a prayer of thanks at this time every year, as I am sure he is healing many other people with fears like me, and hopefully also with a call or text. Thank God for people like Dr. Dave.

A Hat Over the Wall

May 2, 2015 -- I threw my hat over the wall today.

It's a saying I remember, and sometimes use with people who have no idea what I'm talking about, from the Landmark Education Forum, the three-day program designed to bring about life-improving "breakthroughs," which borrowed the phrase from President John Kennedy, who talked about throwing the hat in reference to America's determination to explore outer space, and who appropriated the expression from Irish author Frank O'Connor, who wrote the parable about two adventurous boys who were halted in their journey by an imposing stone wall – until one threw his hat over the top, compelling them both to scale the barrier to retrieve it.

I didn't join NASA; I won't be exploring Mars or spending a year in space. I did register to do (I say "do" rather than "compete in" purposely) the Columbia Triathlon, two hours before registration closed and 15 days before race day after debating whether to commit for a few months. I threw my hat over the triathlon wall.

As the original rap artists Sugar Hill Gang sang in "Rappers Delight": "I don't mean to brag. I don't mean to boast (But we like hot butter on a breakfast toast)." But I guess this is a little about boasting. Anyone who tells others he is doing a triathlon is boasting, prima facie. I am not an avid triathlete. Not like those eccentrics you see with the really tight onesies with the front zipper, the Terminator-style Ray-Bans, the spokes-less, flyaway bikes, the nutrition diaries, the hairless legs (OK for women), the oddly ubiquitous black wetsuits, the de rigueur upmarket bike racks, the fanny belts, the clacking bike shoes, the 8 percent body fat and taut-as-power-cables leg muscles, and the neatly arranged race day gear and supplies, enough to suffice for a week's vacation.

I am an amateur. I train the minimum. I'm not a member of any triathlon club or training group. I flaunt the convention. My ego requires me to do that. If I had all the proper equipment and clothing – *if I looked like a triathlete* -- how could I explain finishing in the bottom 15 percent?

I'm positive I have the oldest and slowest bike of all the competitors...errr...participants: a 12-speed Fuji touring bike I bought in 1984. 1984! I can't give it up, even if it would increase my speed by 20 percent and save my legs. It's part of my carefully crafted image of the anti-triathlete triathlete. My bike pedals have no clips; just old-school straps. I don't lock in with bike shoes. That's unheard of in triathloning. Someone recently recommended I get the clips and the shoes. Solid advice, but I'm not going to – would ruin the image.

I'll likely be one of the few not wearing a wetsuit. Again, bad for the image. I'm going to freeze my ass off at the beginning of the swim.

I train alone and modestly, mostly during lunch breaks at work when I swim or jog. I recently hooked up with another multi-sport event participant for a few bike rides, the one who advised about the bike clips.

Whenever I told him to ride at his own natural pace during our rides, he blew me away and had to wait for me at the nearest stop sign. He also told me about the weekly "bricks" the Mid-Maryland Triathlon Club sponsors – bike rides followed by runs. I love the term. I'm going to put in one or two "bricks" before the event, by myself, just so I can say that I "bricked."

Since I first started doing triathlons, I've averaged – hmmm, let's see – two per decade. (You thought I'd say something crazy, like 10 per year, right?). I did two in the 1980s, and three in the 1990s. I may have never done one again, except I broke my leg in a soccer game in 2012. It was a long and arduous rehab and recovery. I started on the road back by swimming. Then I added cycling. For motivation, I threw my hat over the wall and entered the 2013 Columbia Triathlon. Running was the hardest. I added that last and slogged through a bare minimum of training jogs.

One year and 22 days after surgery for a broken tibia and fibula – and nearly 15 years since my last triathlon -- I completed the Columbia Triathlon, a .93-mile lake swim, 25-mile bike and 6.2-mile run, in 3 hours, 37 minutes. I was proud of that. I had to disappear into the woods for a few minutes to shed some tears over the struggle of the previous year. I was amazingly consistent, too (i.e., consistently slow for a triathlete), finishing in the 85-90 percentile for each leg.

It was a spiritual experience. That's all it is to me now, more than an athletic event. Time? I don't care about time. I'm not chasing anything, not trying to qualify for anything, not seeking a PR (personal record) or age group award. I entered again for the spiritual experience. I want to find a rhythm in the swim and enjoy the feel of warming up in a cold, open body of water. I'll revel in the feeling of speed and the sights and smells of the countryside on the bike. I'll embrace the challenge of the hilly run and find inspiration in the struggle.

I may even break out the Ruggler during the run. That's the Runner-Juggler (the "Joggler" was already taken). Now that may be showing off, but it has a real purpose – refocusing my mind from the pain, monotony and seemingly interminable length of the run to the three airborne balls.

The triathlon is the thrill of being alive, the delight of being able to do it at all. I'm excited I get to go retrieve my hat.

Beware Serious Triathlete
With Full Bladder on Bike

I occasionally poke fun at Serious Triathlete, because, well, they're so grimly serious about the sport. Maybe that is a defense mechanism because I would really like to be Serious Triathlete, grinding relentlessly like a cyborg, but instead I am Occasional Back of the Pack Triathlete, and proud of it. I've completed the Olympic distance Columbia Triathlon two of the past three years, finishing somewhere in the 80th to 90th percentile.

But this article from Active online newsletter explains why I know I will never attain membership in the exclusive club of Serious Triathlete: "Ask a Coach: Does Everyone Pee on Their Bike?"

While the article acknowledges that "not everyone pees on the bike" – I'm glad to tell readers I'm in that category – apparently many racers do.

"The act of peeing while riding is a challenge for most athletes and can take some practice," the coach writes. Wow, I didn't know in addition to practicing swimming, biking, running and transitions, I should also experiment with and perfect methods for relieving myself while on the bike seat!

"If you choose this option, be mindful of other racers around you," the coach continues. I am not kidding; the coach really advises this. Hell, yes, be mindful of the other racers! Lordy Be, that's just common courtesy! I don't mind a spray from a hose

while on the bike, but only a garden hose, not any kind of hose!

"Other options include stopping at a Port-a-Potty or stopping to pee in your tri shorts," the coach says. A Port-a-Potty, what a concept! I vote for that. Or how about in a bush or behind a frickin' tree, dogs do it all the time and the arbor seems to survive. The coach forgot all about those options.

Finally, the coach says, *"Use water from your water bottle to wash off."* Wait a minute. Isn't the whole point to drink your water over time to avoid dehydration, not to use it to dilute the stench in your tri shorts-cum-diaper?

Look, Serious Triathlete, I don't know about you, but I'm going to give up two minutes here and there in a race that takes me three and a half hours to avoid relieving myself in my shorts and riding in discomfort and wretched stench. For me, that may make the difference in finishing in the 84th percentile vs. the 86th percentile. I won't be disappointed.

Unless you have a serious chance of winning some category or scoring some cash prize or qualifying for the Hawaii Ironman or the Olympics, I suggest you do the same. Save your shorts, your bike seat and your washing machine. Don't make your family members and friends cringe and gag from being around you at the post-race celebration; the sweat and grime from a dirty lake swim will be all they should have to tolerate. Don't consider your pee-soaked tri shorts a badge of honor. You'll get a finisher's medal to hang around your neck. That should suffice.

DISCLAIMER: I apologize to any Serious Triathlete who I may have offended...as long as you apologize to me if you pee in your shorts anywhere close to me in a race!

Ode to a 33-Year Relationship That Ended Badly

She was a love of my life. We had 33 wonderful years together, from young adulthood well into midlife. But in the end, she got old, and her body, especially the most important parts, just wore out. Things loosened and sagged. Her usual sharp edges dulled. Midlife is unforgiving in that way. And she hurt me, cut me like a knife. I'm still scarred from our relationship.

Ultimately, I just had to let her go. Our relationship had been broken; she was damaged goods and couldn't be fixed without making wholesale changes. I wish I could say I let her go gently, but that would be a lie. I discarded her like a piece of junk on a scrap heap, and never looked back. I knew she could easily be replaced with a better version that would make me feel safer, happier and livelier, maybe even younger, and eliminate my doubts and anxiety.

Though the ending was brutal, particularly for her, that should in no way invalidate the great times and adventures we enjoyed together, where we essentially operated as one finely-tuned unit.

We first got acquainted as college sweethearts, as I was entering my senior year. We got familiar with each other during those innocent times, spending weekends together in the idyllic small towns, rolling hills and farms of Upstate New York.

Over the next decade, she was a constant companion. We would travel together through the Montana and Canadian Rockies, sleeping under the stars and a light August snowfall; down the rugged Washington and Oregon coasts; amid tropical Florida barrier islands and quaint Vermont towns; and on long, carefree journeys through the Shenandoah, Blue Ridge and Great Smoky Mountains. We enjoyed history together as well, touring the Gettysburg battlefields. We even competed together in triathlons, when she was in better shape than this last, disheartening year.

At home, she was always a loyal, steady and reliable partner. She was always there to pick me up, ready to go when I needed to escape for a while, to clear my head, seek a change of scenery or just relax and re-energize. For decades, I counted on her and returned her loyalty, even as I saw my contemporaries trade in their mates for younger, sleeker models. I admit to having envy, but I stuck by mine, perhaps stubbornly for too long.

Alas, all good things do come to an end. My longtime companion started giving me trouble last spring. Something was wrong with her, just wasn't herself anymore. She became unreliable, nearly left me stranded a few times. Physically, she was breaking down, severely testing my patience. I took her to a specialist, and his prognosis was dire. The decline was irreversible without a major intervention.

Still, I decided to give her one more chance when others might have justifiably called it quits, taking her to Bethany Beach, DE with me for a summer 2017 of teaching tennis. We survived together for a while, but I was wary and it was touch-and-go whenever we spent time together. In short order, she let me down again. It was the last straw. I'd had enough. The relationship was irretrievably broken.

The grey Fuji Del Rey 12-speed touring bicycle that I had purchased for just more than $300 in 1984 had a drivetrain system that was worn and no longer functioning properly. The drive chain had become stretched and the gear teeth were dulled. If the pedal revolutions became too slow for the gear, the chain would detach from the gear teeth and the bike would become inoperable. Going up hills became an adventure, like in the movie *Speed*, where if the bus slowed to less than 50 mph a bomb on board would detonate. If I had to push too hard on the pedals, the chain would click...click...click...and fall off, leaving me on the side of the road trying to reattach the chain, hands blackened with grease.

The beach terrain is flat, so I thought I could milk one last summer out of my Fuji. On a backroads ride, I slowed too much for the gear I was in, and the chain detached. I reattached the chain, but apparently on the wrong gear ring. When I stepped on the pedal to start the wheels rolling, the chain detached and my leg crashed down onto the gear teeth, leaving me with six cuts running up my right leg, a perfect imprint of the gear ring. I managed to reattach the chain correctly and ride another five miles home without incident, but bloodied. Months later, I still have the scars.

That was our last ride together, me and my ancient Fuji. I brought it home on a one-day trip back to Maryland and left it, where my wife unceremoniously placed it on the curb for trash pickup. I don't know if a trash hauler saved her for a new life or crunched it into mangled metal. Either way, I didn't care anymore. We had a past together, but I was over her. Me and Fuji, we were just so...yesterday.

Country Roads, Take Me Home

January 22, 2016 -- A blizzard is supposed to hit the DMV (District of Columbia, Maryland and Virginia) today. I'll finally have to put my bike away.
I lost a job in October 2015. Quit, resigned, fired, laid off, mutual parting of the ways – it doesn't really matter how you phrase it. I was on the unemployment line as a midlife man, not necessarily by choice. But it was for the best. It has allowed me to focus on ramping up my graduate program in counseling and focusing more time and attention on my internship.

Still, the last few months on the job and its loss were stressful. To cope, I engaged in Cycling Fridays, taking most of the day off from other activities to travel to Carroll County, Maryland, bordering on Pennsylvania, to ride routes through backroads, rolling hills, farmland and small towns.

I have nostalgia for Carroll County, a largely rural and agricultural county that has been steadily suburbanizing. I worked there for four years as a reporter for *The Baltimore Sun*, covering agriculture, small towns and county government. I visited dozens of farmers in picturesque settings, writing stories about droughts, dairy operations, beef cattle, breeding, hog farming, farm wives, spring plantings and soybean production. I always loved the country roads and the scenery.

After my job loss, I thought I would make one trek back to my old stomping ground and hang it up for the season. But the weather stayed mild, so I returned for a second Friday. The calendar turned to November, and I thought for sure my Cycling Fridays would be numbered. But November was often positively summer-like, with temperatures in the 70s, so I continued. December would surely be the end.

But December turned out to be a record-warm month for the area, by far: The average temperature was 51.2 degrees, 11.5 degrees warmer than normal, and 5.5 degrees warmer than the previous warmest December. So on Christmas Day, I was back in Carroll County, cycling in my shorts, temperatures in the 60s. It rained that day – hard – but I didn't care. How can you complain about riding a bike outside in the Northeast on Christmas day? I had the whole county to myself that day, there wasn't a soul outside.

All told, I made seven cycling pilgrimages, lifting my spirits through near-weekly rides along creeks, past barns and grazing cows, into valleys, through village outposts that time forgot and over hills with panoramas of endless farmland and the Blue Ridge Mountains at the crest.

I saw a few interesting sights along the way: The guy with the tricked-out, burgundy and gold Washington Redskins pro football car with the gold wheel rims and the "F Dallas" license plate, a reference to the Redskins' longtime rival Cowboys; the front yard sign hanging from a tree reading, "Welcome to Redneck Paradise;" and a ghostly Used Car lot that could have employed the creepy Norman Bates, proprietor of the Bates Motel in "Psycho."

I'm resigned to the chill and shutdown of the approaching blizzard, but glad that it held off long enough for me to rejuvenate my mind, body and spirit from the devastating blow of unexpected job loss.

CHAPTER 14

Creative Expressions and Passions
The Writing Life

When "Someday" Came: A Novel Idea

I just accomplished a big life goal, one of those that you say you are going to do "someday" and that "someday" often never comes. Someday came on April 16, 2015, when my first novel, *Three Yards and a Plate of Mullet,* was published and posted on Amazon.

Writing the book was half the battle, the first offensive. But if I want it to get out in the world, I will have to embark on a publicity and marketing blitzkrieg to cover all flanks, and, yes, self-promotion.
But maybe my story can inspire someone else who is still thinking about that great accomplishment or effort or plan they will make "someday" in the indeterminate future.

I had thought about writing a book for all of my adult life, but never very seriously, at least not seriously enough to ever determine or commit to what exactly I would write about or to draft a first sentence. As I got further into midlife, that lack of commitment began to bother me. You can't call yourself a writer if you don't write; you can't call yourself creative if you create nothing. It's just unrealized potential.

If you do write, you may find out you are not a writer – at least not a novelist/author, the way you believed you were – so it may be safer not to write so you can maintain your self-perception or self-delusion that you are. It's the same with many things: the fear of failure can prevent you from trying, which can serve to preserve your self-image.

On many bus rides home from work, I began thinking seriously about *actually starting* a novel or possibly a non-fiction book, with a growing sense of now-or-never urgency. It was dawning on me that "someday" may never come, and that I was just a fraud (as an author, at least). I mulled over several ideas on the bus, and in the first act of commitment, sketched out some plot ideas for two novel concepts.

I finally decided on one, because I knew it best. The novel would be based on my days as a sportswriter in Florida, my first job out of college, where I covered intense seasons of high school football in a football-mad community and lived a typical bachelor life with other guys at the same stage, except in a tropical environment.

Three Yards and a Plate of Mullet is about a 22-year-old sports fanatic from up North, who lands a job in an insular, foreign community down South, and soon runs up against the region's power broker, the intimidating coach of the perennial high school football powerhouse, who just may have masterminded a school redistricting conspiracy to keep his team on top, and the eccentric characters the sportswriter meets along the way.

In real life, when I first set foot on a deserted Florida high school football field on a scorching preseason August 1985 day, I remember thinking two things about my new adventure: *"Where the heck am I?"* and *"Someday this would make a good novel."*

One day on a Christmas break from work in 2011, I went to the library, intending to start writing, but came home with nothing. Later during that break, I wrote my first two paragraphs longhand. I didn't wind up using those paragraphs, but that was my breakthrough. For me, it's like running: The hardest part is putting on the clothes and getting out the door.

I decided to start with a prologue – setting up the story line of the book with what came before. That allowed me to basically write about my youth and everything that led to me becoming a sportswriter without having to make up much fiction yet. It worked, it got me writing. I also had an idea for some action in the first chapter that would set the scene and the plot of the book, and wrote that next. After I wrote those parts, I gained a sense of possibility.

Writing the book was a long grind, and anything but a straight line. I had only a vague outline of how the story would go, and made up a lot as I progressed. I wrote a lot of it in pieces, not in sequence, and then looked for ways to connect the parts and make transitions.

Time was a big factor. My workday commands 11 hours, including commuting time. That left weekends and weeknights, when I was already physically tired and tired of sitting in front of a computer. I also had just started a graduate school program.

But I started getting good at squeezing in bits of writing whenever I had the chance. I wrote half or more of the book longhand during my bus commutes to and from work. I also wrote in airports, planes and hotels while on travel, while "watching" my daughter's half and full marathons, at work in the lunch room, and on Capitol Hill while killing time before a work event. A few months into my effort, I broke my leg in a soccer game. I became depressed, to the point where I lost inspiration to write, and became consumed with rehabbing and just trying to get through my workdays. It was several months before I could motivate to resume.

All told, it took three years to complete a draft, about 111,000 words. One of the most challenging parts was trying to remember what I had written a year or two earlier to make sure the plot would make sense and there weren't errors in consistency. It had seemed like an interminable project until the last four months or so, when I sensed that I could actually finish. I powered through a lot of writing during two weeks off of work. I can see how a lot of people may start something like this but never finish – it's a commitment to persistence and a long time for a payoff.

I went the self-publishing route, which took about three months – it was more important to me to publish, and in a timely way, not sell.

But I sure do want to sell now. Someday is here.

12 Things I Learned from Writing and Self-Publishing My First Novel

12 simple lessons I learned, and am still learning, through writing my first novel, *Three Yards and a Plate of Mullet.* The story follows an overmatched, rookie sportswriter in Florida covering a season of high school football in a football-mad, semi-backwater town who runs up against a powerful coach from a dynastic family who just may have orchestrated a bribe to get the best athletes redistricted to his school.

1) If you have difficulty adopting long-term views or goals, try to adapt or don't bother starting.
2) There is such a thing as "powering through" with willpower when it comes to writing; it's just a different type of pain.
3) Taking public transportation to work is a good way to get a lot of writing done.
4) You don't have to plan out your whole plot and every detail – but having a basic idea of a story sequence helps speed the process.
5) One of the hardest things about fiction-writing was remembering details about plot, characters and scenes that were written one or two years prior, to ensure story lines and plot connections were logical and to avoid sloppy errors.
6) The Chicago Manual of Style is more a hindrance than a help in many instances.

7) It's a good idea to have Beta readers for pre-publication feedback. I didn't, but will next time.

8) Writing a self-published novel as a first-time, unknown author is an extremely difficult way to make money, so you better have a passion for the act and the process.

9) I didn't realize the importance of having or building a "platform" to market and sell a novel, but now that I've self-published, it appears essential for success.

10)   I'm glad I self-published despite much popular wisdom that says only traditionally published novels optioned by an agent bestow credibility on the novel and author. Publishing house acquisition is a long road to hoe, and immediate gratification rather than posthumous glory was my desire.

11)   The discipline that is most important in writing a novel is...discipline.

12)   There are many people in the U.S. Very few care that you wrote a book. It's your job to find a few more who will care...then a few more, and a few more.

Striving for '*A Big Agenda*' Instead of '*A Small Life*'

In 2014, just after turning 50, I pursued a dream – for the second time – of running for political office, this time for Maryland state delegate. In 2016, I published a nonfiction book recounting the rollicking, 10-candidate free-for-all campaign that some observers called a "circus," and taking a look at the dog-eat-dog, mucky, incestuous, narcissistic business of politics from the trenches. Don't Knock, He's Dead: a Longshot Candidate Gets Schooled in the Unseemly Underbelly of American Campaign Politics, would "amuse some and infuriate others," wrote a local political blogger and campaign strategy consultant who reviewed the book.

Here is the story of how I came to enter this exhilarating yet disillusioning political world, and an excerpt from Don't Knock, He's Dead describing my final push over the precipice of reservation and into the tangle of the state race.

A Midlife Wham-Bam Combo: Job Loss and Divorce

I was 42 years old, and midlife was slamming me hard, hurricane-force winds compelling me to grip a light pole tight lest my legs blow out from under me and hurtle me adrift. For the second time within two years, I had been laid off from a public relations job with a nonprofit organization because of budget cuts amid a post-9/11 World Trade Center terrorist attack economic slump.

Following the second layoff, I entered the Baltimore City Teacher Residency program, seeking a new challenge to do something more meaningful at midlife, an opportunity to make lemonade with the lemons I was accumulating. I taught elementary school in low-income communities. I struggled to survive the torrent of urban education: The needs were great; the resources and support meager; the kids lagging woefully behind and a handful to manage. I met with the principal, who emphasized if I didn't commit to the task with every ounce of energy, I would drown. I contemplated for a night, and accepted reality: Mentally and emotionally, I was half in, half out. The next day, I submitted my resignation, jumping ship from my fledgling teaching career with no life preserver.

Only four months earlier, I had separated from my wife, headed for divorce, with two young kids. I was both free and free-falling.

When I quit my teaching job, it was just short of a year before the next election, and the dormant thought of running for political office surfaced. It was one of those bucket-list things, something I didn't want to go six-feet-under without having attempted.

As a reporter for the *Baltimore Sun,* I covered a largely rural county's political delegation to Maryland's state legislature. It was my first glimpse of citizen legislators up close. The part-time lawmakers were provincial men, long-established and well-respected in their tight-knit, small-town communities—a tire shop owner, a gentleman dairy farmer and banker, a pharmacist, a Realtor, a stock broker. Covering them alerted me it was possible for regular folk to ascend to political office and become bedrock representatives. I wondered if I could do what they did. Anyway, it was a moot point as a journalist; the two endeavors couldn't be intermixed.

It wasn't until I transitioned into public relations eight years later that the light bulb came on. As community affairs director for a social services agency, I organized political forums for state candidates. Observing the forums, I thought that I could perform as well as many of the inexperienced, run-of-the-mill candidates. The seeds were planted; they didn't germinate for another few years, until I was left blowing in the wind, unemployed and on the path to divorce.

Maybe I would have time to campaign while I looked for a job, I thought after bailing out of the Baltimore City classroom without a parachute. I didn't know if it was a life raft to cling to or a bold dream to fulfill, or both. Meanwhile, I obtained a communications position at a health insurance giant—far from a dream job, but a consistent paycheck. Instead of waning, however, the idea of running for council fortified, even with that new lifeline.

I knew the Democratic county council member from my suburban Baltimore district had fallen out of favor. I gathered my courage and filed as a candidate to challenge him. Soon after, the incumbent announced he was resigning before completing his term – *a sign from God?* I thought. Maybe the idea wasn't so quixotic after all. A county Democratic Committee would interview applicants and make an appointment to complete the term.

It was almost a great break—except that the one other officially registered candidate had run and lost against the departing councilman in the previous election and since had become a connected political insider. The insider with a track record was selected.

One and Done?

In that 2006 Democratic county council primary, I ran a bare-bones campaign against the newly appointed councilman with party backing. I lost, garnering 34 percent of the vote—respectable for a late-arriving political no-name who couldn't check the prerequisite boxes as stepping stones. I had not "paid my dues" or built my political network.

I received compliments during the campaign from insiders about my potential and encouragement to stay involved and build upon my effort. I didn't. Life intervened: an aggravating divorce, a new girlfriend, young kids, aging parents, a stressful job. I figured the newly elected council member would become entrenched, and he did, ultimately serving the maximum three terms. The desire didn't burn intensely enough, and I faded from the political scene.

I was satisfied to have given electoral politics one shot in midlife, so I wouldn't spend the rest of my life wondering whether I had the courage to run and what it would be like to put myself into the court of public opinion, to expose myself for all to judge and render a verdict. I had closed that chapter and had no plans to return. I'd sworn it off, closed the door—but left it unlocked. I was occasionally reminded by friends about my run and was asked if I was going to run again, as if I really was a dyed-in-the-wool politician. My answer was no…followed by the caveat that allowed for a sliver of possibility: *But I never say never.*

Seven years later, the perfect storm conspired to compel me to open the door again, when all three Maryland state delegates representing my district announced they were retiring from office, an unprecedented exodus leaving a gaping hole in a business where participants typically solidify their vise grip on power like the Jaws of Life tearing the roof off a car.

The Dream II Takes Shape (Excerpt from *Don't Knock, He's Dead: a Longshot Candidate Gets Schooled in the Unseemly Underbelly of American Campaign Politics)*

The momentum toward registering as an official candidate was growing in my own mind, yet I still hadn't talked to anybody about my intentions…I knew the time had come for a Come-to-Jesus moment with my wife Amy.

"I'm thinking of running for state delegate," I blurted over dinner, and braced for a catapult of mashed potatoes.

"What? Are you serious? Where did that come from? When did you decide that?"

"I'm just thinking about it, checking it out. I haven't decided."

"When were you going to tell me?"

"Tonight. I just did."

"I've supported you in a lot of things before, when you quit your teaching job and when you ran for council and when you went back to school. I don't know if I can support this."

My proposition had landed like a Biggest Loser contestant's balance beam dismount.

"How will you have the time?" Amy asked. "You complain about not having enough time to do things you want to do now."

"I'll just use whatever time I have. Maybe it won't be enough time, just some time."

She had a good point, but I didn't care about such logic or practicality. The idea had taken root, and it had grown hardy, and I couldn't prevent its development. Like a cocaine addict, I knew I was too far gone to stop.

My council run in 2006 was an easier sell. Since our relationship was new, I had decided I was going to run for county council no matter Amy's opinion, and Amy would have to adapt—or leave if she really didn't like it. It was an early test of our relationship, whether we could support each other's goals. Seven years later, it was harder to take such an uncompromising position since we were married. I didn't feel I could be as cavalier—and maybe self-centered—anymore. There's no 'I' in 'Team' mister, Amy would rib me cornily when I was all about me, which was often.

Still, I countered Amy's reflexive dismay at the idea by expressing concern about being controlled and giving *up dreams for my life. Amy and I were fundamentally different. She valued safety, security and predictability. I felt restless and stifled without risk, ambition, challenging goals and freedom.*

I Want The Real Life

At 50 years old, I wanted the freedom to live life my way, like Sinatra crooned, the freedom to make my own choices and to live with the consequences of success or failure. A midlife crisis? No. I didn't give a crap about a red Porsche or Botox injections. But I did feel the clock ticking on the time I had to do meaningful things with my life. What was I going to wait around for? A heart attack? Dementia? Retirement? I don't even play golf. I had the nagging sense, as John Cougar Mellencamp sang in The Real Life, that opportunities to grab the "gold ring"—hell, even bronze—would be continually dwindling:

My whole life
I've done what I'm supposed to do
Now I'd like to maybe do something for myself...
I guess it boils down to what we did with our lives
And how we deal with our own destinies
But something happens
When you reach a certain age
Particularly to those ones that are young at heart
It's a lonely proposition when you realize
That's there's less days in front of the horse
Than riding in the back of this cart

YOLO

As I pondered launching a campaign, my sense of urgency about life heightened. A month after my 50th birthday at my daughter Rebecca's high school graduation, the student commencement speakers referenced the new buzzword "YOLO" —You Only Live Once. They were right, of course, but what can a teenager realistically know about YOLO? It's not until we've had dreams dashed, experienced bad luck and bad timing, suffered life's tragedies, disappointments, cruelties and failures, come to terms with our own limitations, and battled against becoming stultified or buried in mediocrity and tedium that some of us truly embrace the YOLO creed. Much more than failure, I feared regret. I subscribed wholeheartedly to the saying that you will not regret the things you did; you will regret the things you didn't do…

Courage

Some people told me about the courage it takes to run for public office. It might take a certain kind of courage to expose oneself to public scrutiny and judgement, step into the spotlight and put reputation and ego on the line. But I never thought of running for public office as something that requires real courage. To me, real courage defines people who put their lives on the line, military members who defend our country and liberate other people, or police officers, firefighters and other rescuers. Or teachers who face the toughest challenges in the roughest school districts. Or people who take a stand despite risks and public condemnation, whistleblowers and civil rights activists such as Martin Luther King, Jr., Nelson Mandela and Harvey Milk. Or people who are unflappable and unstoppable in the face of abuse, tragedy, disease or disability.

A Hat over the Wall

For me, entering a political race was more like throwing a hat over the wall. "Throwing a hat over the wall" was the metaphor used by President John Kennedy, referring to America's determination to explore space and land a man on the moon. Kennedy appropriated the expression from Irish author Frank O'Connor, who wrote a parable about two adventurous boys who were halted in their journey by an imposing stone wall—until one threw his hat over the top, inspiring them both to scale the barrier to retrieve it. For me, it was crossing the line from consideration to commitment— throwing my hat over the wall...

I drove to a nondescript, red-brick State Board of Elections office in Annapolis, threw my hat through the third-floor window and, for a $50 fee, filed my official registration papers as a candidate...

A Big Agenda

I had told my 17-year-old daughter Rebecca, who had just started college, about my plans the day before registering. She was supportive. The same day I talked to my 15-year-old son and budding computer scientist Daniel about being my "Chief Technology Officer" —a cool title that wasn't to be found on the state registration forms. Daniel already knew about my potential candidacy; he had helped me shoot a video promoting a single-payer health care system.

I knew I couldn't rely on either of my teen-agers to be big-time volunteers, with one in college and each with big academic loads and teen social lives. More importantly, I hoped I could serve as a model for striving for something meaningful, accepting a challenge, and being bold in life—maybe even a little courageous. They had seen me run for county council as 10- and 8-year-olds and had enthusiastically passed out literature to voters on primary election day. Now they had more maturity and wisdom to understand what being a political candidate meant and what it entailed. Still, they were baffled by why I would want to do such a thing, viewing it as another one of dad's quirky "adventures," like when I pulled them on a sled through two feet of snow and over snow banks a mile-and-a-half to Blockbuster, or when I suggested going to a remote, mountainous West Texas national park for Christmas. Regardless their involvement and the outcome, I wanted them to know and remember that I had a dream and wasn't afraid to pursue it, that I strived for a Big Agenda instead of settling for a Small Life even though success was a longshot.

Guitar Hero

At neighborhood events, I often see my former guitar teacher, my neighbor and has a guitar studio within walking distance where I once took lessons. And then, inevitably, a wave of regret and guilt washes over me.

I feel compelled to tell him every time that though it seems like I quit, that I really haven't. No, not me, no quit in this mule. I haven't given up, at least not in my mind. I'm just on a long, long hiatus. He humors me and listens, probably thinking, "Yeah, sure, I've heard that line before." But I'm serious.

I'd love to be able to play guitar well. I surf YouTube videos of guitar performances and marvel at the seeming ease with which the musicians strum and pick, no need for sheet music. What a thrill it would be, I imagine, to play some kick-ass rock song before an audience with both hands working instinctively to reach the right notes and chords.

But that's skipping right over those pesky factors of study, practice and work, the disciplines required to develop a skill, no matter if one is highly or modestly talented. Author Malcolm Gladwell promotes the "10,000 Hour Rule," stating that 10,000 hours of deliberate practice is required even by the most talented to become truly masterful at a craft or skill. At the one studio recital sponsored by my teacher in which I performed, I verged on Choke City, getting through my piece shakily.

My original inspiration to pick up the guitar goes back 25 years. I had a friend who took guitar lessons.

It struck me that I was missing out by not being able to play a musical instrument. I regretted quitting the clarinet as a kid after playing through 6th grade. Music is one of those things that's easier to learn as a child than as an adult. I remember playing in the Holiday concert and feeling like I had the songs mastered.

I quit playing in school mostly because I didn't like having to carry the instrument back and forth. Lame excuse, but my parents didn't force me to continue.

A decade after my friend introduced me to the idea, a colleague's husband donated guitar lessons for a fundraiser auction. I bid and won the lessons, and stayed on as a student for several months. But then the usual excuses intervened -- work, time constraints, two young kids, a 30-minute trip to the teacher's house -- and I stopped. Not quit. Stopped temporarily. Someday, I vowed, I would pick it up again.

Flash forward eight more years. When we discovered we lived in a guitar teacher's neighborhood, we signed up my 12-year-old son Daniel for lessons. Aha, a chance for redemption! Soon after, I signed up as well.

It was clear Daniel had more aptitude than me, and/or his youth enabled him to develop skills faster. He performed at several recitals, and skillfully played more complex pieces than I could master. As it turns out, college freshman Daniel is strong in math and computer science, disciplines that emphasize patterns, sequences and intervals, and have correlations to music. But he lacked passion and commitment. He didn't want to practice, and though I encouraged him, I didn't force him.

About 18 months into his lessons, he announced he wanted to quit. As much as I tried to convince him about his high talent level, and the opportunities he could have if he continued progressing, it didn't change his mind. It was like having a conversation with the young me, determined to quit the clarinet because I couldn't envision the benefits. I hope Daniel returns to guitar some day on his own desire. The talent is there.

I continued with the semi-monthly lessons until the night nearly five years ago when I broke my leg in a soccer game. I had become proficient enough to play a book of 20 Easy Pop Melodies by bands such as the Beatles, Rod Stewart and Kansas, just for fun. But I discontinued lessons during my recovery, and lost motivation to practice as a situational depression set in. I never got back to it. I had just started my 5 1/2 year run in a graduate program, and, you know...the usual excuses.

I still have my guitar -- actually, Daniel's guitar -- and the lesson and song books. I took the guitar to the beach last summer for my seasonal gig teaching tennis, vowing to pick it up again. But the guitar stayed in its case.

Practicing an instrument is something like exercising. The hardest thing about running for me is stepping out the door. With guitar, it's putting the music sheet on the stand and taking the guitar out of the case.

April 26, 2017 marks the five-year anniversary of my broken leg and surgery, which signaled the end of my guitar progress. It would be a good day to take the guitar out of its case again. I haven't quit. I'm just waiting for the right time -- any time except the 12th of Never.

About the Author

ADAM GORDON SACHS is a mental health counselor in Charleston, South Carolina. He holds a master's degree in clinical mental health counseling from the Pastoral Counseling program at Loyola University-Maryland. While at Loyola, he worked in counseling internships with low-income populations in inner-city Baltimore and suburban Washington, and with people with addictions. He transitioned to counseling after working in public relations for health care and social services organizations. He worked as a journalist, including as a sports reporter for the *Sarasota (FL) Herald-Tribune* and news reporter for the *Baltimore Sun.* He has run twice for political office in Maryland at the county and state levels. He holds a master's degree in journalism from Boston University and a bachelor's degree in international relations and history from Colgate University.

He is the author of two other books, the novel ***Three Yards and a Plate of Mullet***, based on his experiences as a rookie sportswriter in Florida, and the nonfiction ***Don't Knock, He's Dead: A Longshot Candidate Gets Schooled in the Unseemly Underbelly of American Campaign Politics***, based on his experiences as a Maryland state political candidate. He writes a blog on midlife issues at: **www.midlifedude.wordpress,com**. He has two children, a daughter and son.

www.ingramcontent.com/pod-product-compliance
Lightning Source LLC
Chambersburg PA
CBHW051733250726
48659CB00001B/36